TAROT
CLASSIC

TAROT CLASSIC

STUART R. KAPLAN

U.S. GAMES SYSTEMS, INC.
Publishers
Stamford, CT 06902 USA

OTHER BOOKS BY THE SAME AUTHOR

TAROT CARDS FOR FUN AND FORTUNE-TELLING

THE ENCYCLOPEDIA OF TAROT

Library of Congress Catalog Card Number: 74-183028

ISBN 0-913866-05-9 (Hard Cover)
ISBN 0-913866-17-2 (Soft Cover)
ISBN 0-913866-55-5 (Gift Set)

The card designs from the Tarot Classic deck are reproduced by permission of Muller & Cie, Switzerland.

PRINTED IN THE UNITED STATES OF AMERICA

Dedicated
To My Wife
Marilyn
and To Our Children
Mark, Peter
Michael, Christopher
and *Jennifer*

Acknowledgments

Grateful appreciation is extended to the many persons who assisted in the completion of this volume, especially

Janet Bennett
> for her tireless efforts in the preparation of the manuscript;

Albert Field
> for assistance in authenticating and verifying many rare tarot cards;

Edwin Nigg of Muller & Cie, Switzerland
> for bringing to production the beautiful pack of Tarot Classic cards.

Preface

When and where did tarot cards originate? What are the meanings of the symbolic pictures? How does one spread and read the cards? Do the cards really foretell the future? I have sought in this volume to provide answers to these and many other questions constantly asked about tarot cards, while opening up new vistas for tarot card appreciation.

Since there are a variety of acceptable explanations as to the origin of tarot cards, I have furnished the reader with the more plausible possibilities. I have also placed special emphasis on the development of the tarot pack, the manner of spreading the cards, the meanings of each card and the methods of interpreting the symbolic pictures as practiced in fortune-telling during the past several centuries. Sample readings described in Chapter VIII illustrate the facility with which one may read the cards.

More books have been written about tarot cards than all

other playing cards combined. Unfortunately, the books about tarot almost inevitably deal only with the fortune-telling aspects of tarot packs. Scant mention is made of the artistic tarot prints, as used in the game of tarock, which present a pictorial history of the events, the arts, and the life styles of both nobility and commoner through the centuries. This book will attempt to acquaint the reader with the many types of tarot cards generally unknown to the user of tarot for fortune-telling.

Most of the original scholarly works about tarot dating from the 18th and 19th centuries are inaccessible today. Court de Gebelin's treatise "Du Jeu des Tarot" published in 1781 in *Le Monde Primitif* is virtually impossible to find. Singer's *Researches into the History of Playing Cards* appearing in 1816 was printed in only two hundred and fifty copies. Duchesne's *Jeux de Cartes Tarot et de Cartes Numérales du XIV au XVIII siècle* published in 1844 was issued in only one hundred and thirty-two copies. I have freely drawn upon these and other rare volumes from my private collection in researching this book.

Also presented are illustrations of some of the many different varieties of tarot cards used in fortune-telling and the games of tarock and tarotrump. Some of the cards shown date from the 15th century such as the Minchiate of Florence cards, the Sforza-Visconti pack from Milan and the Tarocchi of Mantegna cards. Other illustrations include tarot packs currently popularized by U. S. Games Systems, Inc. and Muller & Cie, Switzerland, including the 1JJ Tarot Deck, The Rider Waite Pack as well as the B. P. Grimaud pack known as Tarot of Marseilles.

Known as a collector of rare books on the history of playing cards, especially tarot packs, as well as a collector of the rare original packs of cards themselves, I have occasionally been asked to appear on television and radio and at lectures and press parties to demonstrate the use of tarot cards for fortune-telling. It might be well to state at this point that I personally do not employ tarot cards for fortune-telling in my personal life. The primary fascination that the cards hold for me is as mysterious pieces of art with substantial, historical background. However, numerous public readings have actually resulted in startling and perceptive results. There is no question in my mind that the proper shuffle and spread of the pack can enable a diviner to read from the cards a perceptive revelation of events almost always clearly associated with the person who shuffled the cards. Yet, in an attempt to maintain an unbiased outlook, I have considered the tarot pack as a work of art, which it is, and I have sought in an objective manner to present the background of facts about the cards as I understand them.

I have been motivated in my work, in part, by the striking lack of factual material available to the public about tarot cards. Most of the recent books deal solely with the fanciful aspects of fortune-telling without revealing the equally interesting and extensive historical background of the cards themselves. While *Tarot Classic* is not intended as an exhaustive treatise upon the subject of tarot, it is a compendium of many facts relating to tarot packs, their origin, development and use. I believe *Tarot Classic* will serve to bridge the gap between the tarot pack as a method of fortune-telling and its historical significance as a work of art expressed in many varieties during the past several centuries.

STUART R. KAPLAN

New York, N. Y.

Contents

List Of Illustrations

CHAPTER V

CHAPTER VI

CHAPTER VII

CHAPTER VIII

BIBLIOGRAPHY

✍◎ CHAPTER I ◎✍
Introduction To
The Tarot Deck

CURRENTLY IN AMERICA there is a phenomenal interest in
ancient European tarot fortune-telling cards. Tarot decks are
sought by students, teenagers, housewives, businessmen, professional people, collectors—indeed, persons in all walks of
life. The serious believer employs the cards for divination, as a
means of placing the past into more meaningful perspective,
understanding the present, and revealing the alternatives
which may exist in the future. Persons less familiar with the
esoteric meaning of the cards are content to use them as a game
and to engage in readings at parties or in small private groups.

Teenagers and students revel in fun-packed parties with
tarot, witchcraft and occult themes. Adults attend tarot
luncheons, charitable benefits and even tarot picnics at which
card readings are demonstrated. There are lectures and
symposiums available for persons seeking serious introduction

to tarot, and libraries and museums, if they are fortunate enough to possess or borrow authentic 16th to 19th century packs, display the rare tarot decks at special exhibits.

Authentically reproduced tarot decks are available in many retail stores throughout the country including stationery, book and greeting card stores, gift shops and boutiques. Many large department stores feature occult departments offering tarot and related products. So-called "mod" and "head" shops offer an endless variety of tarot, astrological and occult-oriented items.

Book stores offer dozens of different tarot titles purporting to unveil the *real* esoteric meaning of the tarot pack. There are also tarot songs, Broadway plays in which the tarot images come alive on the stage, a popular musical featuring the tarot theme, and endless references to tarot in short stories, novels and poems including T. S. Eliot's *The Waste Land.* The popular emblematic tarot designs appear on countless items including fabric designs, posters, souvenirs, greeting cards, games, paintings, collector's plates, jewelry, desk ornaments, key chains, colorful clothing patches, and *objets d'art.*

Newspapers, magazines, radio and television comment frequently on the tarot vogue. A public library in New England issues its annual report on the backs of outsized tarot cards. A large savings bank uses tarot cards in a 30-second television commercial for predicting the best way to make money grow (through a savings account, naturally). Store designers utilize the tarot theme as a back drop for fashions in gaily lit store window displays. A recent millinery trade show used tarot as its merchandising theme for store buyers throughout the country.

Through choice or chance, depending upon one's viewpoint, the twenty-two Major Arcana cards from the seventy-eight-card tarot deck are clearly interwoven into our daily lives.

Some tarot cards have loaned their titles to popular magazines and newspapers. Time or *The Hermit* calls attention to *Time* magazine. Fortune or *The Wheel of Fortune* is symbolic of *Fortune* magazine. The *Star, Sun,* and *World* are well-known newspapers of their day. Each of us gives and needs to receive love as exemplified by *The Lovers.* Astrological influences intrigue many of us as we follow our horoscope in *The Stars.* The influence of *The Moon* beguiles us to the extent that in our generation we witness astronauts exploring the moon's surface. We depend upon, revolve around and there are those of us who worship *The Sun* and its warmth-filled rays. Repeatedly, we are motivated by, and sometimes caught between, life's two great human frailties: love *(The Lovers)* and fortune *(The Wheel of Fortune).* Our fears are concealed during moments of transition as *The Hanged Man* while at other times, in confidence or confusion, we abandon the past in *The Lightning Struck Tower.*

Each of us possesses a touch of the creativity and magic of *The Magician,* a predilection for frivolity as typified by *The Fool* and, on occasion, an undeniable bit of *The Devil* himself. We all have known at one time or another the successful businessman or leader in *The Emperor,* and the dynamic and competent woman of *The Empress.* We meet in our lives, perhaps through religious conviction or by virtue of friendship, the traditionalism of *The Hierophant.* Each of us experiences a moment of admiration, possibly tinged with a vague feeling of discomfort, at the scholarly *High Priestess,* so wise and knowledgeable, yet incapable of any meaningful emotion or expression.

Life is hectic in our current age. As a warrior astride his *Chariot* drawn by two horses pulling apart, we rush towards ultimate failure or triumph, often forgetting the cardinal virtues of *Temperance, Justice,* and *Strength.* Time or *The*

Hermit is our most fleeting possession. Having lived a lifetime in search of our ultimate *World*, we are finally called to the moment of *Judgment*.

Begrudgingly, we slowly realize that each day draws us closer to the final moments of life. Thus, the triumphal processional of the tarot cards continues—from the birth and creation of *The Magician* and the innocence of *The Fool* to the final moments in the card of *Death*.

What is this fascinating and mysterious tarot deck about which so much has been written? The seventy-eight-card tarot deck is divided into two main groups: twenty-two Major or Greater Arcana cards, and fifty-six Lesser or Minor Arcana cards. The Major Arcana or emblematic cards comprise an unnumbered card known as The Fool (counterpart of the Joker in a modern-playing card deck), plus twenty-one cards numbered from I to XXI (1 to 21). Also known as trumps *(atouts* in French, *atutti* in Italian), the Major Arcana cards generally bear the following descriptive titles:

NO.	ENGLISH	FRENCH	ITALIAN
	The Fool or The Foolish Man	Le Mat, Le Fou or Le Fol	Il Matto
I	The Magician, The Juggler, The Thimble-Rigger, The Cup Player, The Mountebank or The Pagad	Le Bateleur or Le Jouer de Gobelets	Il Bagatto or Il Bagattel
II	The High Priestess, The Female Pope, The Popess or Junon	La Papesse	La Papessa
III	The Empress	L'Impératrice	L'Imperatrice
IIII	The Emperor	L'Empéreur	L'Imperatore
V	The Hierophant, The Pope or Jupiter	Le Pape	Il Papa
VI	The Lovers	L'Amoureux	Gli Amanti
VII	The Chariot	Le Chariot	Il Carro
VIII	Justice	La Justice	La Giustizia
VIIII	The Hermit	L'Ermite	L'Eremita
X	The Wheel of Fortune	La Roue de Fortune	Rota di Fortuna or Ruota della Fortuna

NO.	ENGLISH	FRENCH	ITALIAN
XI	Strength, Force or Fortitude	La Force	La Forza
XII	The Hanged Man or The Hanging Man	Le Pendu	Il Penduto or L'Appeso
XIII	Death	La Mort	Il Morte or Lo Specchio
XIIII	Temperance	La Tempérance	La Temperanza
XV	The Devil	Le Diable	Il Diavolo
XVI	The Tower, The Lightning Struck Tower, The House of God, The Hospital, The Tower of Babel or Fire of Heaven	La Maison de Dieu	La Torre
XVII	The Star	L'Etoile	La Stelle
XVIII	The Moon	La Lune	La Luna
XVIIII	The Sun	Le Soleil	Il Sole
XX	Judgment or The Last Judgment	Le Jugement	L'Angelo or Il Giudizio
XXI	The World or The Universe	Le Monde	Il Mondo

Each of the Major Arcana cards bears a descriptive title and a symbolic picture which awakens in the diviner's mind a connected story considering the trend of the cards. The descriptive presentation on each card, except for minor refinement, has remained the same for over five centuries.

The fifty-six Lesser Arcana cards are divided into four suits containing fourteen cards each and corresponding to the suits in an ordinary deck of playing cards:

ENGLISH	FRENCH	ITALIAN	CORRE-SPONDING TO
Swords	Epées	Spade	Spades
Wands, Scepters, Batons or Clubs	Batons	Bastoni	Clubs
Cups, Chalices or Goblets	Coupes	Coppe	Hearts
Pentacles, Coins, Money or Circles	Deniers	Denari	Diamonds

Each suit consists of Ace, two, three, four, five, six, seven, eight, nine, and ten plus four court or dress cards: King *(Roi* or *Re)*, Queen *(Reine* or *Dama)*, Knight or Horseman *(Cavalier* or *Cavallo)* and Jack, Page or Knave *(Valet* or *Fanti)*. Thus, there is an 'extra court card which, in its proper sequence, is positioned between the Queen and Jack.

Today's ordinary four-suit numeral pack of playing cards appears to be a direct descendant of the 14th-century tarot decks. As card playing increased in popularity, the twenty-two Major Arcana cards were dropped, except for The Fool which was retained as the Joker, and the Knight and Page were combined into today's Jack, thus giving us the standard pack of fifty-two cards plus Joker.

Origin Of Tarot Cards

THE PRECISE ORIGIN of tarot cards is obscure. Tarot and playing cards may have had their beginning as long ago as ancient Egypt, since scholars have reportedly recognized the Major Arcana as Egyptian hieroglyphic books. Other scholars, however, report remarkable similarities between playing cards and early Eastern games and deities. Even the much later medieval age cannot be discounted as having presided at the birth of tarot cards. It is not even known with certainty whether the Major Arcana cards with their emblematic designs and the Lesser Arcana cards in their familiar four suits were devised separately and at a later date some inventive genius combined them into one pack, or if they were created as a seventy-eight-card deck from the onset. The following are some of the more plausible explanations as to the origin of regular playing cards and esoteric tarot cards.

Clues to the birth and early development of tarot and playing cards are given here in chronological order. Lastly, references are made to early decks, similar to tarot cards, which were popular in Italy during the 15th century, and progress to the 18th-century Tarot Classic deck.

Egyptian Book of Thoth

Court de Gebelin in 1781 writing in Volume I of *Le Monde Primitif* presents a strong argument in favor of the Egyptian origin of tarot cards. According to Gebelin, the twenty-two Major Arcana cards are an ancient Egyptian book, *The Book of Thoth*, saved from the ruins of the burning Egyptian temples. Thoth was the Egyptian Mercury said to be one of the early kings and the mythical inventor of speech and hieroglyphs or letters with its attendant mysticism. Its basis was an alphabet in which all gods are letters, all letters ideas, all ideas numbers and all numbers perfect signs. Many scholars of the occult recognize in tarot cards the pages of hieroglyphic books, containing the principles of the mystic philosophy of the Egyptians in a series of symbols and emblematic figures. Gebelin believed that the esoteric tarot symbols subsequently were spread throughout Europe by wandering gypsies. In Chapter III we offer further details about some of Gebelin's concepts.

Chess

The ancient Indian game of *Chaturange* or Four Kings bears striking similarities to the four suits of regular playing cards. This oriental game dating from the 5th or 6th century, the forerunner of today's modern game of chess, originally had its King, General (the modern Queen) and Horseman, plus its pawns or common soldiers. There was no Queen originally, as the introduction of a female into a game representing the stratagems of war would have been contrary to oriental ideas of propriety. It is entirely possible that in ancient India a group of players, finding themselves without playing pieces for *Chaturange,* devised on strips of bark or paper similar designs which developed subsequently into a game of its own merit.

Indian Deities

Some ancient Indian playing cards contain either eight or ten suits in a set, and twelve cards to each suit, consisting of

Collection of the Author

Incarnations of Vishnu Shown are four suits representing four of the ten incarnations or avatars of Vishnu, the Indian deity: *(top row)* Tortoise and Fish; *(bottom row)* Boars and Swords. The court cards are heavily lacquered and elaborately decorated. The round cards are 2-5/8" in diameter with plain backs.

numerals 1 to 10 plus two court cards. The suit signs are similar to the ten incarnations or avatars of Vishnu, one of the Hindu divine trinity. The suit signs are:

Incarnation	Name	Suit Sign
First	Matsya	Fish
Second	Kurma	Tortoises
Third	Varah	Boars
Fourth	Nara-simha	Lions
Fifth	Vamana	Dwarfs or Water Jars
Sixth	Paracu-rama	Axes
Seventh	Rama-chandra	Arrows
Eighth	Krishna	Cows
Ninth	Buddha	Shells
Tenth	Kalki	Swords or Horses

The last incarnation, *Kalki*, The White Horse, is yet to come and will usher in the end of the present age. There are numerous variations to the above suit signs and some of them are hard to recognize in Indian playing cards.

China - Chess - Dominoes - Dice

One variety of Chinese cards has the same name as Chinese chess, *Keu-ma-paou* or Chariots-Horses-Guns, which suggest the possibility that the game of cards originally came from Chinese chess.

Chinese dominoes, marked in the same manner as the dice from which they apparently derived, are thought to have been originally used for divination. There are twenty-one distinct pieces, representing the permutations of two dice. Eleven of these pieces are doubled, making a total of thirty-two in the set. It is believed by some researchers that playing cards evolved from dice through the Chinese wooden domino.

Korean Divinatory Arrow

The theory that Korean playing cards are derived from Korean divinatory arrows rests with the eighty-card Korean decks known as *Htou-Tjyen*. These cards are generally strips of oiled paper eight inches long by one quarter inch wide. The backs are uniformly marked with the image of an arrow feather. The decks are divided into eight suits. The card faces appear to be highly conventionalized shaftments of arrows, retaining in their suit markings the same symbolism as that of the quiver of arrows from which they are derived. Thus, there may be some justification in the belief that cards possibly developed from Korean divinatory arrows.

Fez, Morocco

Paul Foster Case, in his book *The Tarot, A Key to the Wisdom of the Ages,* advances the theory that about the year A.D. 1200 a group of scholarly men from all parts of the globe met in the city of Fez, Morocco. In order to overcome their language differences they prepared a pictorial book which became the emblematic pages of the tarot deck, understandable to all the wise men. There is, however, no evidence to support this fanciful theory.

Crusaders

Some scholars believe that playing cards were brought into Europe by the Crusaders. However, the last of the Crusades ended about 1291, and there is no substantive reference to playing cards in Europe until at least one hundred years later.

Gypsies

Many people associate fortune-telling cards with the gypsies, originally of Hindustan origin and driven from India at the beginning of the 15th century by Timur Lenk, Islamic conqueror of much of central Asia and eastern Europe. Gypsies are generally known as card conjurers par excellence, supposedly having a reputation for fortune-telling inherent in their blood.

Gypsy bands began their large westward movement about the year 1400 across the Indus through Afghanistan and the deserts of Persia and along the Persian Gulf to the mouth of the Euphrates. Continuing into the great deserts of Arabia, they found their way to Europe by various routes. Small bands of early drifters were found in Crete, Corfu and the Balkans before 1350. In 1417, a band of gypsies arrived near Hamburg, Germany. Other accounts place the gypsies in Rome in 1422, and in Barcelona and Paris in 1427.

However, the evidence is fairly substantive that the gypsy race did not extend its wanderings into Europe until after cards had been known there for some period of time.

Johannes, A German Monk

A German monk named Johannes, writing at Brefeld, Switzerland, states that "a game called the game of cards *(ludus cartarum)* has come to us in this year 1377," but he expressly states that he was ignorant of "at which time it was invented, where and by whom."

In his handwritten treatise presently in the collection of the British Museum in London, Johannes compares the game of cards with chess "since in both there are kings, queens and chief nobles and common people."

Of the cards used, he says that men "paint the cards in different manners, and play with them in one way or another. For the common form, and as it came to us: four kings are depicted on four cards, each of whom sits on a royal throne, and each holds a sign in his hand."

Viterbo - Covelluzzo - Saracens

A manuscript dealing with the history of Viterbo by Feliciano Bussi, published in 1742, allegedly quotes Covelluzzo, a 15th-century chronicler:

> *"Anno 1379, fu recato in Viterbo el gioco delle carti, che venne de Seracenia e chiamasi tra loro* Naib."

> "In the year 1379, was brought into Viterbo the game of cards, which comes from the country of the Saracens, and is that they called *Naib.*"

Giovanni Covelluzzo wrote his history of Viterbo in 1480. Therefore, since Covelluzzo was not contemporaneous with the date mentioned, it is uncertain whether his reference to playing cards was merely his personal opinion, the personal opinion of one of his ancestors, Nicholas de Covelluzzo, from whose earlier chronicle Giovanni may have extracted the information, or if either had any means to substantiate that cards came from the Saracens, Arabs, or Moors.

Naipes

One of the chief arguments for the Saracenic origin of cards is the Spanish name for playing cards, *naipes,* a word which may derive from the Biscayan *napa,* signifying flat or even.

Some scholars believe the origin of the word *naipes* comes from Arabic. The Hebrew word *naibes* resembles the old Italian name of cards *naibi,* and in both languages it denotes sorcery, fortune-telling and prediction.

Another theory asserts that the word *naipes* is derived from the initial letters of the alleged name of the inventor of cards, N. P. for one Nicolao Pepin, but there is no evidence to substantiate such a conclusion.

Alphonso XI

Alphonso XI, King of Castille, founded in 1332 an order of chivalry called the Band, of which not a vestige exists today. However, Don Antonio de Guevara, Bishop of Mondonedo, published at Valladolid in 1539 in his *Golden Epistles* a copy of the statutes of this order. In a subsequent French translation of these statutes published by Dr. Gutery in 1558 at Lyon under the title *Lettres Familières,* there is a passage to the effect that the knights of the Band were forbidden to play at cards or dice for money. *(Comandoit leur ordre que nul des chevaliers de la Bande, n'osast iouer* [sic] *argent aux cartes où dez.)*

Dr. Gutery does not cite the specific Spanish edition of the epistles which he used but assures us that he translated it from the original text which presumably was a Spanish manuscript. However, the word *cartes* is not to be found in the original Spanish edition by Guevara and therefore no proof exists that playing cards for money was prohibited in Spain by the statutes of an order established in 1332.

John I

John I, King of Castille, allegedly issued an ordinance prohibiting dice, *naipes,* and chess in the year 1387.

Charles VI - Gringonneur

In the accounts book of Charles Poupart, Treasurer to

Charles VI of France, there exists a passage which states that three packs of cards in gilt and variously ornamented were painted by Jacquemin Gringonneur for the amusement of the King of France in the year 1392. Gringonneur was paid 56 sols of Paris.

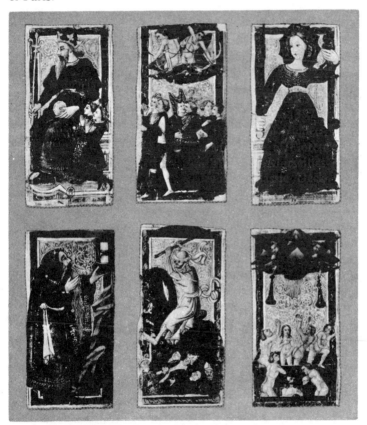

Gringonneur or Venetian Tarot Cards Six of the seventeen so-called Gringonneur cards. Shown left to right, are (*top*) The Emperor, The Lovers, and Justice; (*bottom*) The Hermit, Death and Judgment. The hand-painted cards are sumptuous in pictorial design and belong to a style of the 14th century. Some researchers believe the cards were not painted by Gringonneur in 1392 but instead are of Venetian origin from the mid-15th century.

"Donné à Jacquemin Gringonneur, peintre, pour trois jeux de cartes à or et à diverses couleurs, de plusieurs devises pour porter devers ledit Seigneur Roi, pour son ébattement, cinquante-six sols parisis."

Many persons have thus credited Gringonneur with the invention of playing cards for the purpose of diverting the King's melancholy. However, the passage by Poupart implies nothing more than that three decks of playing cards, already known, were specially painted for the King.

Interestingly, there exists today seventeen cards in the archives of the Bibliotheque Nationale in Paris believed for many years to be the original Gringonneur cards although the cards are probably of 15th-century Venetian origin.

The seventeen cards from the so-called Gringonneur pack are without inscriptions, letters, or numbers to indicate the manner in which the cards are to be arranged. However, they are readily identifiable with modern tarot symbols as well as with ten, perhaps thirteen, designs from the fifty-card Tarocchi of Mantegna pack.

Gringonneur Pack	Modern Tarot	Tarocchi of Mantegna
1) Le Fou	The Fool	**MISERO I**
2) L'Empéreur	The Emperor	**IMPERATOR VIIII**
3) Le Pape	The Pope	**PAPA X**
4) Les Amoureux	The Lovers	**APOLLO XX**
5) Le Chariot	The Chariot	**MARTE XXXXV (?)**
6) La Justice	Justice	**JUSTICIA XXXVII**
7) L'Ermite	The Hermit	**SATURNO XXXXVII (?)**
8) La Fortune	The Wheel of Fortune	**ASTROLOGIA XXVIIII (?)**
9) La Force	Strength	**FORTEZZA XXXVI**
10) La Tempérance	Temperance	**TEMPERANCIA XXXIIII**
11) La Lune	The Moon	**LUNA XXXXI**
12) Le Soleil	The Sun	**SOL XXXXIIII**
13) Le Valet d'Epée	Valet of Spades	**CHEVALIER VI**

Gringonneur - Temperance This card is similar to the symbolic figure of Temperance in modern tarot packs which depicts the essence of life flowing between two vessels. The seventeen so-called Gringonneur cards are said to have been preserved from the collection of M. de Gaignieres, assistant tutor of the grand-children of Louis XIV, who bequeathed them together with his entire collection of prints and drawings to the King in 1711.

The following four subjects have no corresponding figures in the Tarocchi of Mantegna cards; however, they are found among the Major Arcana cards of modern tarot decks.

14) Le Pendu | The Hanged Man
15) La Mort | Death
16) La Maison de Dieu | The Tower
17) Le Jugement | Judgment

Ordinance January 22, 1397

Playing cards are not mentioned in a decree issued by Charles VI in 1369 against gaming, even though many games of hazard are enumerated. Yet, twenty-eight years later, the Prévôt de Paris, in an ordinance dated January 22, 1397, was obliged to "forbid working people from playing tennis, ball, *cards,* or ninepins, excepting only on holidays." Thus, we can place the approximate date of the introduction of playing cards into France as some time between 1369 and 1397, probably closer to the later date.

A number of tarot-type decks appeared in Italy in the 15th century bearing similarities to the seventy-eight-card tarot deck as we know it today.

Tarocchi of Mantegna

The Tarocchi of Mantegna deck, also known as the *Carte di Baldini,* comprises fifty instructive cards in five classes of ten cards each. The cards are listed in a clear order of the universe. The figures in each set of ten cards ascend in orderly fashion from the simplest to the greatest for that category. The sets progress according to number but in the reverse letter order so that the last set, which comprises the order of the planets and
\'s to the First Cause of all things, God, bears the first letter

Tarocchi of Mantegna Cards Ten cards in series E are numbered from 1 to 10 and represent the various ranks of life from The Beggar to The Pope. Two cards, Series D, numbers 11 and 12, represent the Greek muses Calliope and Urania. Card number 1, *Misero*, depicts a beggar being seized at the leg by a dog, similar to *Le Mat* or The Fool in the tarot pack. Note that two cards, *Imperator* and *Papa*, bear titles used in modern tarot packs, The Emperor and The Pope respectively. Other Mantegna cards shown, and the court cards in modern tarot packs which they resemble, include: 2 *Fameio* — Page of Cups, 4 *Merchadante* — King of Coins, 5 *Zintilomo* — Page of Batons, 6 *Chavalier* — Page of Swords, 7 *Doxe* — King of Cups, and 8 *Re* — King of Swords.

SERIES E

I	Misero	The Beggar
II	Fameio	The Valet or Knave
III	Artixan	The Artisan or Goldsmith
IIII	Merchadante	The Merchant
V	Zintilomo	The Gentleman or Nobleman
VI	Chavalier	The Knight
VII	Doxe	The Doge of Venice
VIII	Re	The King
VIIII	Imperator	The Emperor
X	Papa	The Pope

SERIES D

XI	Caliope	Calliope, muse of epic poetry
XII	Urania	Urania, muse of astronomy
XIII	Terpsicore	Terpsichore, muse of dancing and choral singing
XIIII	Erato	Erato, muse of lyric poetry and mime
XV	Polimnia	Polyhymnia, muse of singing, rhetoric and mime
XVI	Talia	Thalia, muse of comedy and pastoral poetry
XVII	Melpomene	Melpomene, muse of tragedy
XVIII	Euterpe	Euterpe, muse of lyric poetry and music
XVIIII	Clio	Clio, muse of history
XX	Apollo	Apollo, god of the sun, prophecy, music, medicine and poetry, and leader of the muses

SERIES C

XXI	Grammatica	Grammar
XXII	Loica	Logic
XXIII	Rhetorica	Rhetoric
XXIIII	Geometria	Geometry
XXV	Aritmetricha	Arithmetic
XXVI	Musicha	Music
XXVII	Poesia	Poetry
XXVIII	Philosofia	Philosphy
XXVIIII	Astrologia	Astrology
XXX	Theologia	Theology

SERIES B

XXXI	Iliaco	Astronomy
XXXII	Chronico	Chronology
XXXIII	Cosmico	Cosmology
XXXIIII	Temperancia	Temperance
XXXV	Prudencia	Prudence
XXXVI	Forteza	Fortitude or Strength
XXXVII	Justicia	Justice
XXXVIII	Charita	Charity
XXXVIIII	Speranza	Hope
XXXX	Fede	Faith

SERIES A

XXXXI	Luna	The Moon
XXXXII	Mercurio	Mercury
XXXXIII	Venus	Venus
XXXXIIII	Sol	The Sun
XXXXV	Marte	Mars
XXXXVI	Jupiter	Jupiter
XXXXVII	Saturno	Saturn
XXXXVIII	Octava Spera	The 8th Sphere
XXXXVIIII	Primo Mobile	The Chief Agent or The Prime Mover
XXXXX	Prima Causa	The First Cause

The British Museum in London possesses an incomplete set of forty-seven cards believed to date from either 1470 or 1485 and there are several other packs at leading museums and in private collections both in the United States and Europe.

Tarocchi of Venice

Tarocchi of Venice or Lombardi decks contain seventy-eight cards including twenty-two Major Arcana and fifty-six Lesser Arcana cards. Venetian tarots introduced the figure entitled *La Papasse*. This symbolic figure is known in subsequent tarot packs as The High Priestess and, around 1800 at Besançon, was changed to *Junon*.

Tarocchino of Bologna

Tarocchino of Bologna decks comprise sixty-two cards and are believed to have been invented by Francois Fibbia, Prince of Pisa, while an exile in that city. He died there in 1419. The pack contains the usual twenty-two Major Arcana cards but only forty numeral suit cards, the pip cards numbered 2, 3, 4 and 5 of each suit having been dropped. Neither titles nor names appear on the cards, whether the Greater Arcana or the court figures. The first four *atutti* are unnumbered, and bear figures of Moors in the place of the Papal and Imperial cards and of the legendary female Pope, probably due to the fact that after 1513 the Republic of Bologna passed under Papal domination. The numeral suits are the usual *spade, bastoni, coppe* and *denari*.

Minchiate of Florence

Minchiate of Florence decks are similar to the regular seventy-eight-card tarot decks but enlarged to ninety-seven cards. There are forty-one trump cards, nineteen of the original series plus the twelve signs of the Zodiac, the four Elements, the three Theological Virtues (Faith, Hope and Charity) and one Cardinal Virtue (Prudence). The first thirty-five cards called *papi* are numbered with Roman numerals and arranged in the following order without titles:

Italian Minchiate Cards The complete Florentine Minchiate pack, (circa) 1670, totals ninety-seven cards. Each card has an extra sheet of paper wrapped from the back around the front edges and bearing a dotted pattern. The unnamed cards shown, left to right, are: (*upper row*) I The Juggler, VI Temperance, XIII Death; (*middle row*) XVI Hope, XXVII Aries the Ram, King of Swords; (*bottom row*) Knight of Swords, Page of Cups, 3 of Coins. The Knights of this pack are chimeric figures composed of human busts on equine bodies. The suit of coins usually depicts heads inside the coins. The full-color cards measure 2-5/16" x 3-3/4" and are square-cornered. Backs are decorated with a floral pattern in dull gray.

I	The Juggler	XIX	Charity
II	The Grand Duke	XX	Fire
III	The Emperor	XXI	Water
IV	The Empress	XXII	Earth
V	Love	XXIII	Air
VI	Temperance	XXIV	Libra, The Balance
VII	Force	XXV	Virgo, The Virgin
VIII	Justice	XXVI	Scorpio, The Scorpion
IX	The Wheel of Fortune	XXVII	Aries, The Ram
X	The Chariot	XXVIII	Capricornus, The Goat
XI	The Hermit	XXIX	Sagittarius, The Archer
XII	The Traitor	XXX	Cancer, The Crab
XIII	Death	XXXI	Pisces, The Fishes
XIV	The Devil	XXXII	Aquarius, The Water Carrier
XV	The Tower	XXXIII	Leo, The Lion
XVI	Hope	XXXIV	Taurus, The Bull
XVII	Prudence	XXXV	Gemini, The Twins
XVIII	Faith		

The next five unnumbered cards, called *arie*, are arranged in the following order without titles: The Star, The Moon, The Sun, The World, and The Last Judgment, sometimes depicted as Fame. The court cards are also unnamed and invariably single-figured. This game probably predates the Tarocchino of Bologna game and bears striking similarities to some of the Tarocchi of Venice cards.

Visconti-Sforza Deck

One of the oldest known decks still in existence today dates from 15th-century Milan. Francesco Sforza, the fourth Duke of Milan, was the original owner of a seventy-eight-card tarot deck known now as the Visconti-Sforza cards. The deck bears the four suits of *spade, bastoni, coppe* and *denari* plus the twenty-two Major Arcana cards including *Il Matto,* The Fool.

The Visconti-Sforza deck was probably painted sometime between the years 1432, when the betrothal of Francesco Sforza and Bianca Maria Visconti united the families, and 1466, the year Duke Francesco died.

Visconti-Sforza Tarot Cards
Three cards from the famous
15th-century Visconti-Sforza
pack, originally owned (circa
1450) by the fourth Duke of
Milan, and presently in the
collection of the Pierpont
Morgan Library in New York
City. The cards shown, unnamed are: (*top left*) Temperance, (*top right*) Queen of
Swords, and (*bottom*) The
Wheel of Fortune. The cards
are handpainted and illumi-
nated on thick cardboard.
The trump and court cards
are painted in brilliant colors
on a diapered background of
gold over red with occasional
spreads of silver used for
armor or in the decoration of
robes. The cards measure
6-7/8" x 3-5/16" and are
square-cornered. The backs
are plain red.

Thirty-five cards of the Visconti-Sforza deck, including fifteen Major Arcana without title or number, were acquired in 1911 by the Pierpont Morgan Library in New York City. Of the remaining cards, twenty-six are in the possession of the Accademia Carrara in Bergamo, Italy, and thirteen cards are held by the Colleoni family of Bergamo. The remaining four cards are missing.

Tarot of Marseilles

By the end of the 15th century the Italian tarot deck had undergone some modifications and throughout Europe, but especially in France, the Tarot of Marseilles deck—somewhat different in design but with identical subjects—became widely popular. The twenty-two Major Arcana and sixteen court cards are single-headed rather than the double-headed figures popular in modern Piedmontese tarot packs. The older tarot packs also used Roman figures rather than the Arabic numbering. Tarot packs, wherever they were produced in Europe, generally bore the titles of the Major Arcana cards in French and continued to use the Italian suit signs of swords, wands, cups and pentacles.

Grimaud Tarot of Marseilles Cards This classic tarot deck in beautiful colors bears the titles of the trump cards in English. These cards are made by B. P. Grimaud of France. The cards are lithographed on heavy quality stock and are round-cornered. The designs are typical Tarot of Marseilles symbols. The cards measure 2-9/16" x 4-7/8". The back design is a connected square design in blue.

THE FOOL   THE MAGICIAN   THE EMPEROR

THE TOWER OF DESTRUCTION   THE CHARIOT   THE WORLD

Tarocchino of Mitelli

Giuseppe Maria Mitelli, an engraver and painter who lived in Bologna, Italy, was born in 1634 and died in 1718.

In the year 1664, Mitelli engraved a series of sixty-two Tarocchino cards comprising four suits of four court cards, the numeral cards 10 to 6 and the Ace, plus twenty-two *atutti* including *Il Matto*. The highest *atutti* is called *Il Giudizio* and the lowest *Il Tempo*. On the Ace of *Coppe* appears the arms of Bentivoglio of Bologna, the family for whom the hand-colored etchings were executed.

Reprinted from Bologneser Tarockspiel

Mitelli Tarocchino Cards Shown are three of the sixty-two cards designed by Mitelli for the Tarocchino of Bologna pack. The *atutti* cards shown represent 2 The Bearded Pope, 3 The Empress and 4 The Emperor. The Empress and The Emperor are depicted as sovereigns of the East and West. In addition, Mitelli changed the female Pope to a second, bearded Pope (not shown) standing, and probably representing the Eastern patriarch. Mitelli took considerable artistic liberties with the usual symbolic designs of the tarot pack.

Mitelli considerably altered the usual representations of the *atutti* or trump cards. For example, the male and female Popes became two bearded Popes, one seated and the other standing, the latter possibly intended to represent the Eastern Patriarch. The Emperor and the Empress also are depicted as Sovereigns of the East and West. The Hanged Man, *Le Pendu,* is replaced by a man striking another with a mallet. The Hermit, usually heavily garbed, becomes a disrobed winged figure of Time on crutches. The Sun and the Moon, artistically treated in the Mitelli prints, are depicted as Apollo, the Greek mythological god, and Diana, the Roman mythological goddess.

The line drawings are delicately executed and the cards representing the Fool and the Magician are especially expressive. Generally, however, the cards are difficult to relate to the traditional Tarocchino symbols. The designs of Mitelli are remarkable for their strange and sometimes ingenious character rather than for the manner in which they are executed.

Tarot Classic Deck

The 18th-century Tarot Classic deck is based upon original woodcuts by Claude Burdel. The Burdel pack contains the usual Italian suit marks and the twenty-two Major Arcana cards. The two of Pentacles bears the inscription: "Claude Burdel Cartier et Graveur, 1751." Appearing on the three of Cups and The Chariot are the initials "C.B." showing that Burdel both engraved and sold the cards. Notwithstanding the portrayal of French arms on the Burdel tarot pack, it is possible that these cards may have been originally issued at Soleure in Switzerland, or its nearby area, since the arms of

I
LE BATELEVR

II
LA PAPESSE

III
L'IMPERATRISE

IIII
LE MPEREVR

V
LE PAPE

VI
LAMOVREVX

VII
LE CHARIOR

VIII
IVSTICE

VIIII
L'ERMITE

X
LA ROVE DE FORTVNE

XI
LA FORCE

Burdel Tarot Classic Cards - Major Arcana The Major Arcana numbers I through XI from the original Burdel woodcuts. The Tarot Classic deck is based upon the Burdel designs dating from 1751. Note the initials "C.B." on card No. VII, The Chariot. The titles of the 22 Major Arcana cards as they appeared on the original pack are: I—*Le Batelevr*, II—*La Papesse*, III—*LImperatrise*, IIII—*LEmperevr*, V—*Le Pape*, VI—*Lamovrevx*, VII—*Lecharior*, VIII—*Ivstice*, VIIII—*Lermite*, X—*La Rove de Fortvne*, XI—*La Force*, XII—*Le Pendv*, XIII—(untitled death card), XIIII—*Tenperance*, XV—*Le Diable*, XVI—*La Maison Diev*, XVII—*Lestoille*, XVIII—*La Lvne*, XVIIII—*Le Soleil*, XX—*Le Ivgement*, XXI—*Le Monde* and *Le Mat*.

France also appear on prints from this canton, owing probably to Soleure having been the place of residence for many years of the French ambassador to the Swiss Republic. The Tarot Classic cards illustrated in Chapters IV and V of this book are based upon the designs of Claude Burdel with slight modifications by the artists at Muller & Cie, Switzerland.

Burdel Suit of Pentacles The four court cards in the suit of *deniers* or pentacles from the original Burdel woodcuts. The figures are designated *Roy* (King), *Reyne* (Queen), *Cavallier* (Knight) and *Valet* (Page). The four of Pentacles bears an eagle in the shield and the two of Pentacles carries the inscription: "Claude Burdel, Cartier et Graveur, 1751."

Tarot And Tarotée Etymology

The origin of the word tarot, much like the origin of the cards themselves, remains obscure. Some scholars believe the word derives from Egyptian dialects. Others regard the word tarot as evolving from the term *tarotée* which was applied to the back design of early cards bearing a multiple series of criss-crossing lines in varying widths similar to the back design presently used on the Tarot Classic deck.

Tarotée Design

Other early cards were occasionally bordered with a silver margin on which were represented a spiral band formed of fine dots or points. These small dots or imitated holes were known as *tares,* and cards having them were called *tarots* or said to be *tarotées.*

The word tarot has been said also to have been derived from the games of *tarocchi* or *tarocchino* to which we have previously referred.

In the statutes of the guild of card makers of Paris in the year 1594, the cartiers call themselves *tarotiers,* another form of the word tarot.

There exists in the possession of a small number of private collections a limited number of authentic tarot decks and tarot-type cards dating from the 15th to 19th centuries. These exceedingly rare original decks are treasured by collectors and occasionally can be purchased by individuals interested in tarot.

ᴄ🙠 CHAPTER III 🙡ᴐ

Development Of Tarot Cards

Court de Gebelin

Antoine Court de Gebelin was born in Nimes in 1725 and died in Paris on May 10, 1784. He studied theology at Lausanne and followed his father, Antoine Court, as a pastor of the Reformed Church.

Gebelin was an ardent scholar of ancient mythology. Involving himself in the study of religions from the standpoint of linguistics, he sought to rediscover the primitive tongue whose hieroglyphic writing would explain the various known mythologies, all of which supposedly reflect in symbols the same revealed truths.

Gebelin devoted twenty years to his vast research and then set forth his ideas in nine volumes, published in Paris from 1775 to 1784 entitled: *Le Monde Primitif, analysé et comparé avec le monde moderne.* In Volume I, commencing at page 363, Gebelin presents a dissertation entitled: *"Du Jeu des*

33

Collection of the Bibliothèque Nationale, Paris

A. Court de Gebelin

Tarots. Ou l'on traité de son origine, où on expliqué ses allegories, et où l'on fait voir qu'il est la source de nos cartes modernes à jouer, etc, etc." Gebelin advances the theory that tarot cards are of Egyptian origin and should be regarded as an Egyptian book which comes down to us through the centuries as an epitome of the Egyptian doctrines on some important and interesting topics.

According to Gebelin, tarot cards were either an allegory expressed in ancient Egyptian hieroglyphics relating to their philosophy and religion, or a book presenting the history and creation of the world and of the first three ages, commencing with Mercury himself. The four suits were meant to represent the four states or orders of political society. The whole foundation of the tarot cards was resolved from various aspects into the number seven which was sacred to the Egyptians and upon which they based the elements of all sciences. Each suit or color was composed of twice seven cards. The *atouts* number three times seven, and the total number of cards is seventy-seven, The Fool being "0." The gypsies, according to Gebelin, were in fact Egyptians who dispersed over Europe and from whom we derive the custom of fortune-telling with cards. Gebelin saw the word tarot as a combination of *tar* signifying way or road, and *ro, ros,* or *rog,* implying king or royal; the word tarot meaning, therefore, the "royal road of life."

"Imagine the surprise that the discovery of an Egyptian book would cause," wrote Gebelin, "if we heard it said that a work of the ancient Egyptians still existed in our time—one of the books saved from the flames which consumed their superb libraries—and which contained their purest beliefs regarding interesting things. Everyone would, no doubt, be eager to know such a precious and extraordinary book. If we added that this book is in very general use in a large part of Europe and that it has been in the hands of everyone for a number of centuries, it certainly would be surprising were it to be believed. Wouldn't it be the greatest surprise, if we vouched that we have never suspected that the book was Egyptian, and that we own it without really owning it because we have never tried to decipher one page of it, or to look upon the fruit of its exquisite wisdom as anything more than the accumulation of foolish figures meaning nothing in themselves? Wouldn't it be thought that we are trying to insult the intelligence of this audience?

"This Egyptian book does exist," asserted Gebelin. "This Egyptian book is all that remains in our time of their superb libraries. It is even so common that not one scholar has condescended to bother with it since no one before us has ever suspected its illustrious origin. This book is composed of seventy-seven, even seventy-eight sheets or pictures, divided into five classes, each showing things which are as varied as they are amusing and instructive. In a word, this book is the game of Tarot, a game, unknown in Paris, it is true, but very well known in Italy, Germany and even in Provence. This game is bizarre because of the kinds of figures appearing on its cards as well as their great number.

"Regardless of the countries in which they have been used, there has been no further progress made on the value of the odd figures which this game appears to offer. And its ancient origin is such that it has been lost in the shadows of time so that we have not known either where or when it was invented, nor the theme around which so many extraordinary figures have been assembled, figures nearly too disparate to go together and representing in their entirety an enigma which no one has ever tried to resolve.

"This game has even appeared so little worthy of attention that it has never been considered by those of our scholars who have been studying the origin of cards. They have never spoken of anything but French cards—or what was used in Paris—the origin of which is not very old. And after having proved them to be a modern invention, they have believed that they have exhausted the matter. In fact, we continually confuse whatever information we have with the country of its original invention. We have already shown this with regard to the compass. Even the Greeks and the Romans have overly confused these things which have deprived us of a great deal of interesting information."

Gebelin tells us that it was only by chance he came across mystical tarot cards. "Invited to go call, a few years ago, on a lady who knew some of our friends, Madame the Countess of H..., who had arrived from Germany or Switzerland," relates Gebelin, "we found her busy playing this game with a few other people.

'We are playing a game which you surely do not know.'

'That may be. What is it?'" [inquired Gebelin]
"'The game of Tarot.'
'I had the occasion to see it played when I was very
young, but I know nothing about it.'
'It is a rhapsody of the most bizarre, the most absurd
figures; here is one for example.'

"She took care to choose the one most loaded with figures,
and even though it did not bear any resemblance to its name,
said, 'It's the world.'

"I glanced at it and as soon as I did, I recognized the
allegory. Everyone put down his hand and came to look at this
marvelous card in which I saw what they had never before
seen. Each person showed me another card, and in a quarter of
an hour the deck had been gone through, explained and
proclaimed Egyptian. And since this was not a figment of our
imagination, but rather the result of selected and sensible
knowledge of this game in connection with everything that was
known about Egyptian ideas, we promised ourselves to surely
make it known to the public one day; we were convinced that it
would be pleased to have a discovery and a gift of this
kind—an Egyptian book which has escaped barbarism, the
ravages of time, accidental and spontaneous fires and ignorance which is still more disastrous."

Gebelin resolved to explain the allegories on the cards and to
show that the ancient, wise Egyptians had known how to
convert their most useful knowledge into amusement by
making it into a game. "The game of Tarot is composed of
seventy-seven cards (perhaps even of seventy-eight) divided
into trumps and suits. The trumps which number twenty-two
represent in general the temporal and spiritual leaders of
society, the physical powers of agriculture, the cardinal

virtues, marriage, death, and resurrection or the Creation; the various games of fortune, the sage and the fool, time which consumes all, etc. Thus, we see that all these cards are also allegorical pictures relative to all of life and capable of unlimited combinations."

Gebelin also described the allegorical meaning of the four suits: "Apart from the trump, this game is made up of four suits represented by their signs. They are called Swords [épées, piques, spades], Cups [coeurs, hearts], Batons [trèfles, wands, clubs], and Coins [carreaux, pentacles, deniers, money, diamonds]. Each of these suits consists of fourteen cards, the cards numbered from 1 to 10 and four face cards which we call the King, Queen, Knight and his Equerry or Knave."

Gebelin ascribed the four suits to the four classes into which the Egyptians were divided.

> The sword represented the sovereigns and all the military nobility.
> The stick or the club of Hercules represented agriculture.
> The cup represented the sacerdotal rank, clergy or priesthood.
> The denier represented commerce of which money is the sign.

Gebelin firmly concluded that the game of tarot, therefore, must have been invented only by the Egyptians since it is based on the number seven; it pertains to the division of the Egyptians into four classes; most of its trump are definitely connected with Egypt such as the two chief Hierophants, male and female (equivalent to II The High Priestess and V The Hierophant), Isis or the Dog-Star (XVII The Star), Typhon (XV The Devil), Osiris (VII The Chariot), The House of God (XVI The Tower), The World (XXI The World), the dogs

Gebelin Tarot Cards Six of the Major Arcana cards which accompanied Court de Gebelin's famous work published in 1781 *"Du Jeu des Tarots"*. Shown are: XVII *Lestoille*—The Star, XVIII *La Lvne*—The Moon, XVIIII *Le Soleil*—The Sun, XX *Le Jvgement*—Judgment, XXI *Le Monde*—The World and *Le Mat*—The Fool. Note the close similarity between these designs and the corresponding cards in the Tarot Classic deck.

which guard the tropics (XVIII The Moon), etc.; and since the game was entirely allegorical as one might reasonably expect from a study of Egyptian art and philosophy.

The origin of the card designated The High Priestess or The Female Pope has always been subject to considerable conjecture especially in view of its obvious displeasure to papal authorities. The answer may lie in the fact that the heads of the Egyptian sacerdotal rank were permitted to marry, and the designation in 16th-century European tarot packs of *La Papasse* may merely represent a poor extrapolation from ancient times.

Gebelin traced the route which tarot took to reach Europe. "During the first centuries of the church, the Egyptians were very close to Rome and they gave it their ceremonies and the cult of Isis and as a result the game which concerns it. This game, interesting in itself, was limited to Italy up until the time of its union with Germany [Holy Roman Empire] when this nation learned about it; and up until the time of the union of the counts of Provence with Italy and especially the stay of the court of Rome at Avignon which introduced the game into Provence and Avignon.

"If it did not get as far as Paris," says Gebelin, "we must attribute it to the strangeness of its figures as well as to the volume of cards which were hardly of a nature to appeal to the vivacity of French ladies. It eventually became necessary to greatly reduce the size of the deck in order to accommodate them. Yet, Egypt itself no longer benefits from its invention. It has been reduced to the most deplorable slavery and the deepest ignorance and has been deprived of all the arts so that its inhabitants would be hard put to produce one single card of this game.

"If our French cards, which are infinitely less complicated, necessitate the sustained work of a multitude of hands and the combination of a number of arts, how could this unfortunate people be expected to be able to maintain theirs? Such are the evils which befall an enslaved nation that it even loses its forms of amusement. But since it was not able to preserve its most precious advantages, by what right could it lay claim to something which was only a pleasant pastime?"

As further proof of the oriental origin of tarot, Gebelin cites the oriental names of Taro, Mat and Pagad. "As previously described, the word *Taro* is pure Egyptian representing the royal road of life. It refers, in fact, to the total life of the citizens since it is made up of the different classes into which they are divided. And this game is with them from birth until death showing them all the virtues and all the physical and moral guides to which they should cling, such as the king, the queen, the leaders of religion, the sun, the moon, etc. It teaches them at the same time, through the thimble-rigger and the wheel of fortune, that nothing is so transitory in this world as the various states of man. It teaches them that their sole refuge is in virtue which never is lacking when needed.

"Mat, the vulgar name for fool which still exists in Italian, is from the oriental *mat* meaning senseless, battered, cracked. Fools have always been represented as being crack-brained.

"Pagad, is called the thimble-rigger, in the course of the game. This word, which resembles nothing in our western languages, is truly oriental and very well chosen. *Pag* in the orient means leader, master, lord, and *gad* means fortune. In fact, he is shown as if he were disposing of fate with his Jacob's stick or magician's wand."

Gebelin thus unveiled the mystery of the tarot pack and for nearly two centuries his followers and admirers have ardently expounded and developed his theories.

Etteilla

One of the ardent followers of Gebelin was a man who proceeded to promote Gebelin's ideas to garner great fame and fortune.

Alliette, described alternately as a wigmaker and a Professor of Algebra, was a clever opportunist with great imagination. He reversed the order of the letters of his name giving it a more uncommon sound and, as Etteilla, became absorbed in the theory of numbers according to the system of Pythagoras, a Greek philosopher of the 6th century B.C., who expounded a theory of the description of reality in terms of arithmetical relationships.

Etteilla published many writings of his revelations including, in 1783, his famous work: *Manière de se récréer avec le Jeu de Cartes nommées Tarot.* "We may well be astonished," wrote Etteilla, "that time which destroys, and ignorance that changes everything, should have allowed a work composed in the 1828th year of Creation, 171 years after the Deluge, and written 3953 years ago, to have descended to our own times. This work was produced by seventeen Magi, including the second of the descendants of Mercury—Athotis; who was grandson of Cham, and great-grandson of Noah; this Tri-Mercury (or third of the name), decreed the Book of Thoth in accordance with the science and the wisdom of his ancestors."

Etteilla knew how to capture the imagination and minds of the populace of his time. He adapted the tarot pack to his own system and promoted cartomancy to its fullest. He sought to be as precise and as scientific as his imagination would allow.

The wigmaker, Alliette, thus became the high priest of religion, Etteilla, the great diviner, *Le Célèbre Etteilla.* He installed himself in the Hôtel de Crillon on Rue de la Verrerie

Grand Etteilla Tarot Cards The Fool, instead of appearing as the first card, is placed in the Grand Etteilla pack as the last card, number seventy-eight. The Etteilla designs represent a departure from the standard symbolic pictures found on most other tarot cards. The designs on the emblematic cards are mostly full-length figures. The titles are double-ended and vary to take into account reverse meanings. The cards shown and their corresponding tarot equivalents: 5 Voyage or Earth—The World; 8 Etteilla or Lady Consultant—has no tarot equivalent; 17 Death or Nothing-ness—Death; 38 Arrival or Dishonesty—Knight of Cups; 50 Man of Law or Wicked Man—King of Swords; 78 Folly or Mad-ness—The Fool. The cards are lithographed by B. P. Grimaud of France on heavy stock and measure 2-9/16" x 4-11/16". The cards are square-cornered and the backs bear a connected square design in blue.

in Paris and his following surpassed all imagination. During the perilous days of 1789 he forebode the fate of many. Frenchmen who would fall victim to the events of the times.

The tarot cards of Etteilla, known as The Grand Etteilla cards, are a set of emblematic cards based on the designs of the typical tarots and accompanied by a numeral series, beginning with number 1, *Etteilla questionnant,* to number 78, *Folie,* the whole being equal in number to an earlier Venetian tarot sequence of seventy-eight pieces. The marks of the suits of the numerals are *batons, coupes, épées,* and *deniers.* The designs on the emblematic cards are full-length figures. The court cards, also full-length figures, hold in their hands the signs of their suits. Some of the cards are accompanied by astronomic and astrologic signs. Above and below each design is a title and each card is numbered in its upper left-hand corner. The Aces are always a human hand and part of the arm holding the sign of the suit.

Although the Etteilla designs are significantly modified from the customary tarot symbols, the following comparisons will indicate the similarities between certain cards.

ETTEILLA CARD   EQUIVALENT TO TAROT SYMBOL

NO.	TITLE	NO.	FRENCH	ENGLISH
1	Questionnant			
2	Feu	19	Le Soleil	The Sun
3	Eau	18	La Lune	The Moon
4	Air	17	L'Etoile	The Star
5	Terre	21	Le Monde	The World
6	Jour			
7	Protection	?	?	?
8	Questionnante			
9	Justice	8	La Justice	Justice
10	La Tempérance	14	La Tempérance	Temperance
11	La Force	11	La Force	Strength
12	La Prudence	? 12	Le Pendu	The Hanged Man
13	Mariage	6	L'Amoreux	The Lovers

NO.	TITLE	NO.	FRENCH	ENGLISH
14	Force Majeure	15	Le Diable	The Devil
15	Maladie	1	Le Bateleur	The Magician
16	Jugement	20	Le Jugement	Judgment
17	Mortalité	13	La Mort	Death
18	Traitre	9	L'Ermite	The Hermit
19	Misère	16	La Maison Dieu	The Tower
20	Fortune	10	La Roue de Fortune	The Wheel of Fortune
21	Dissension	7	Le Chariot	The Chariot

This set of cards, designed and arranged for the purposes of divination by Etteilla, was accompanied by a book of explanations and directions, bearing the title: *Manière de tirer. Le Grand Etteilla où tarots Egyptiens.* In the *"Notions Préliminaires"* with which the book commences, it is stated that *"L'art de tirer les tarots* is an agreeable science and of exciting interest, but its results become serious or recreative, miraculous or frivolous, in a ratio with greater or lesser degree of faith possessed by those who resort to it. It is a pursuit that merits especially the confidence of amateurs, particularly female ones, who are so partial to secrets."

There are available today authentic reproductions in beautiful full color of the original Etteilla cards.

Eliphas Levi

Whereas Gebelin and Etteilla earnestly sought to prove the Egyptian origin of tarot cards, Eliphas Levi believed tarot cards were a sacred and occult alphabet attributed by the Hebrews to Enoch, the oldest son of Cain, by the Egyptians to Hermes Trismegistus, the Egyptian god of Thoth, and by the Greeks to Cadmus who founded the city of Thebes.

Eliphas Levi was a philosopher and a profound symbolist. His real name was Alphonse Louis Constant, and he was an Abbe of the Roman Church. However, for his philosophical and occult writings, he translated his name into Hebrew, Eliphas Levi Zahed, and he became known as Eliphas Levi.

Levi found in the tarot a synthesis of science and the universal key to the Kabbalah. He wrote in his famous work, *Dogme et Rituel de la Haute Magie:* "The tarot, this miraculous book, the source of inspiration of all the sacred books of the ancient peoples, is the most perfect instrument of divination that can be employed with entire confidence, on account of the analogical precision of its figures and its numbers. In fact, the oracles of this book are always rigorously true, and even when it does not predict anything, it always reveals something that was hidden, and gives the wisest counsel to those who consult it."

Levi recognized that the Tree of Life in Kabbalism contains twenty-two paths by which the Sephiroth or Numerations are connected, one with another. Later interpretations of Kabbalism married these paths to the twenty-two letters of the Hebrew alphabet. Levi proclaimed that the twenty-two Major Arcana cards should be rightly attributed to each of the letters in the Hebrew alphabet thus constituting a complete unity of letters, cards, and paths.

Levi was enthralled by the tarot meanings he perceived. He stated, "As an erudite Kabbalistic book, all combinations of which reveal the harmonies preexisting between signs, letters, and numbers, the practical value of the tarot is truly and above all marvelous. A prisoner devoid of books, had he only a Tarot of which he knew how to make use, could in a few years acquire a universal science, and converse with an unequalled doctrine and inexhaustible eloquence."

His book, *Dogme et Rituel de la Haute Magie,* is divided into two separate parts, *dogme* and *rituel,* being theory and practice. Each part has twenty-two chapters, one each for the twenty-two trumps, and each chapter deals with the subject represented by the picture depicted on the trump. However, the numeral designation of the chapters to the cards is incorrect. Some occult scholars believe that Levi felt himself bound by his original oath of secrecy to the Order of Initiates which had given him the secrets of the tarot and for this reason he purposely confused the sequence. Other scholars, with justification, regard this viewpoint as an excuse rather than a satisfactory explanation.

The key to Levi's revelation "is contained in a word, and in a word of four letters: it is the *Tetragramma* of the Hebrews, the *Azot* of the Alchemists, the *Thot* of the Bohemians or Gypsies, and the *Taro* of the Kabbalists. This word so variously expressed implies *God* and signifies *Man* to the philosopher, and offers to adepts the last word of human sciences, and the key of Divine power. But he alone knows how to employ it who understands the necessity of never revealing it.

"When the Sovereign Priesthood ceased in Israel, when all the oracles of the world became silent in presence of the Word which became Man, and speaking by the mouth of the most popular and gentle of sages, when the Ark was lost, the sanctuary profaned, and the Temple destroyed, the mysteries of the Ephod and Theraphim, no longer recorded on gold and precious stones, were written or rather figured by certain wise kabbalists first on ivory, parchment, on gilt and silvered leather, and afterwards on simple cards, which were always objects of suspicion to the Official Church as containing a dangerous key to its mysteries. From these have originated those tarots whose antiquity was revealed to the learned Court de Gebelin through the sciences of hieroglyphics and of numbers, and which afterwards severely exercised the doubtful perspicacity and tenacious investigations of Etteilla."

Collection of the Bibliothèque Nationale, Paris

M. Le D'Encausse (Papus)

Papus

Gerard Encausse (1865-1917), a learned French physician who wrote under the occultist name of Papus, contributed significantly to the occultism of tarot and the assimilation of the twenty-two trump cards of the tarot deck to the twenty-two letters of the Hebrew alphabet.

The Rota Wheel

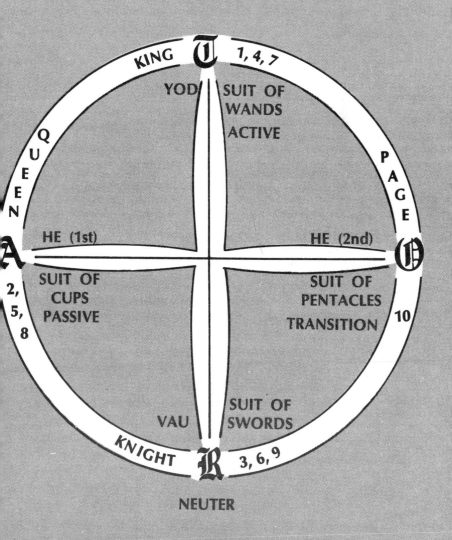

KING ᴛ 1, 4, 7

YOD / SUIT OF
WANDS

ACTIVE

QUEEN

PAGE

HE (1st)   HE (2nd)

SUIT OF
CUPS

PASSIVE

SUIT OF
PENTACLES

TRANSITION

2, 5, 8

10

SUIT OF
SWORDS

VAU

KNIGHT ᴋ 3, 6, 9

NEUTER

The founder and leader of the spiritual and masonic Order of Martinist as well as a member of the Kabbalistic Order of the Rose-Cross, Papus believed that the dominant characteristic of teaching in ancient India and Egypt was its synthesis, which condensed into a few simple laws the whole of acquired knowledge. In the ancient world, knowledge was only transmitted to those men whose worth and confidence had been proven by a series of tests. This transition took place in the temples, under the name of Mysteries, and the adept assumed the title of Priest or Initiate. This science was secret and occult and from this esoteric practice we derive the name Occult Science. However, a time approached when the Initiates feared that their doctrines might be lost to humanity and, according to Papus, they made strenuous efforts to save the law of synthesis from oblivion by passing on this information through three methods:

1. Secret Societies. These organizations were to serve as a direct continuation of the mysteries.
2. The Cultus. This was a religious cult seeking to translate the one existing religion to the different nations according to their particular temperaments. Each cultus had its tradition, its book and Bible.
3. The People. Lastly, it was believed that the people would transmit from generation to generation through succeeding ages the special wisdom and knowledge hitherto only known to the Initiates. This oral law is called the Kabbalah, from a Hebrew word which signifies that which is received, that which comes from elsewhere, that which passes from hand to hand.

Papus based his occultist philosophy on a form of Kabbalism which employs a mysticism of numbers as they relate to names and letters. The basis for his philosophy lies in the theosophic doctrine concerning the Divine name YOD, HE, VAU, HE = JEVE = JEHOVAH. This is known as tetragrammaton whereby the YOD, shaped like a comma or dot, represents the principle or origin of all things and all the other letters in the Hebrew alphabet are formed from this symbol. The YOD is also the symbol of the Ego and the Unity principle. It corresponds in the tarot to the suit of Wands or Scepters and to the Kings of the court cards.

The HE, the second letter, represents the passive in relation to the YOD which symbolizes the active or the Non-Ego in relation to the Ego. HE thus signifies the substance in contradistinction to essence. It corresponds in the tarot to the suit of Cups and the Queens in the court cards.

The VAU, the third letter, signifies the link or affinity that subsists between the first two letters and it completes the root idea of the Trinity. It unites the active to the passive. It corresponds to the suit of Swords and the Knights in the court cards.

The second HE marks the passage or transition from one world to another. It represents the complete Being, comprising in one Absolute Unity the three letters which compose it; Ego, Non-Ego and Affinity. It corresponds to the suit of Pentacles and the Knaves in the court cards.

Whereas the whole tarot is based upon the word ROTA arranged as a wheel, the YOD, HE, VAU, HE can also be represented in the same drawing as indicated below. Papus further developed his law of numbers to each of the twenty-two Major Arcana cards and the forty pip cards.

The concepts and application of Papus' codices and diagrams are presented in his famous work: *The Tarot of the Bohemians. Absolute Key to Occult Science.*

The Kabbalah

The Kabbalah, a system of religious philosophy dealing with the mystical apprehensions of God, holds that creation was accomplished through emanation and thaumaturgy. The theosophy of the Kabbalah follows along the lines of pantheism, the doctrine that equates God with the forces and laws of the Universe.

Christian D. Ginsburg, writing in his work *The Kabbalah, Its Doctrines, Developments and Literature* published in 1863, tells us that the Kabbalah was first taught by God Himself to a select company of angels who formed a theosophic school in Paradise. The angels eventually communicated this heavenly doctrine to the disobedient children of the earth, to furnish the protoplasts with the means of returning to their pristine nobility and felicity. From Adam it passed to Noah and then to Abraham, the friend of God, who emigrated with it to Egypt where the Patriarch permitted a portion of this mystical doctrine to be revealed to the Egyptians and other eastern nations.

Another version contends that the Kabbalah was given directly by God to Moses during his forty days stay on Mount Sinai and, through its mysterious science, Moses allegedly was able to solve the many difficulties which arose during his management of the Israelites. Moses initiated the seventy elders into the secrets of this doctrine and they in turn transmitted them by word of mouth. Moses also covertly laid down the principles of this secret doctrine in the first four books of the Pentateuch (Genesis, Exodus, Leviticus and Numbers) but withheld them from the last book, Deuteronomy.

The Kabbalah is also referred to as *Secret Wisdom* because

it is handed down from the Initiated and it is indicated in the Hebrew scriptures by signs which are hidden and unintelligible by those who have not been instructed in its mysteries.

There are two ancient books which treat with the doctrines of the Kabbalah; the first and oldest book, *Sefer Yezira*, is helpful in order to understand the doctrines enumerated in the second book, the *Sohar*, which presents the concept of the "thirty-two ways of secret wisdom" and the arrangement of the Tree of Life.

Sometime after A.D. 100 there appeared in Babylonia an esoteric book called *Sefer Yezira* (also *Sefer Yetzira*, and *Sefer Jetzira*). This *Book of Creation* or *Book of Formation* sought to exhibit a system whereby the Universe might be viewed in connection with the truths given in the Bible, thus showing, from the gradual and systematic development of Creation, that One God produced it all and that He is over all. The twenty-two letters of the Hebrew alphabet were used, both in their phonetic sense and in their sacred character, as expressing the divine truths of the Scriptures. However, since the Hebrew alphabet is also used as numerals, which are represented by the fundamental number ten, this decade was added to the twenty-two letters of the alphabet and the sum total of thirty-two numbers was designated the "thirty-two ways of secret wisdom." The fundamental ten, divided into a tetrade and hexade, were shown as the gradual development of the world out of nothing. At first there was nothing but the Holy Spirit, at the head of all things and represented by number 1 of the tetrade. Subsequently, the entire Universe proceeded in gradual and successive emanations, the air, number 2, emanating from the Spirit; water, number 3, proceeded from the air; and ether or fire, number 4, emanated from water. Each unit of the hexade represented space in six directions, the four corners of the world (east, west, north and south) and height and depth

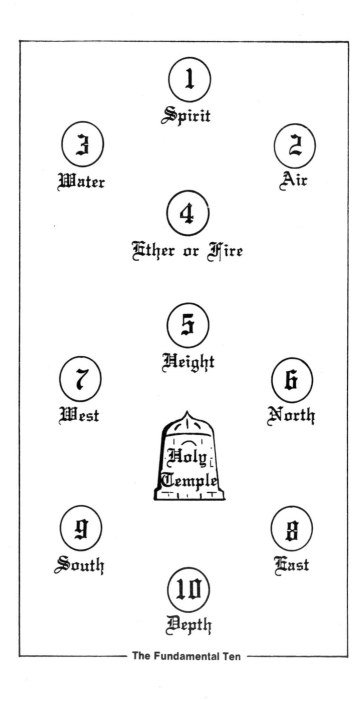

The Fundamental Ten

which emanated from each other. In the center of these manifestations is the Holy Temple supporting the whole.

Following the primordial number 10, from which the whole Universe proceeded, there were the twenty-two letters by means of which God, having drawn, hewn, and weighed them, and having variously changed and put them together, formed the souls of everything that has been made, and that shall be made.

The twenty-two letters of the Hebrew alphabet were then divided into three groups: (1) the three mothers or fundamental letters; (2) seven double letters; and (3) twelve simple consonants, thus establishing a triad of elements, a heptade of opposites, and a duodecimo of simple things as illustrated in the following chart:

Twenty-two Letters of Hebrew Alphabet

Three Mothers	Seven Double Letters	Twelve Simple Letters
Fundamental Letters	Consonants	Consonants
Aleph	Beth	Vau
Mem	Gimel	Cheth
Shin	Daleth	Heh
	Kaph	Zain
	Peh	Teth
	Resh	Lamed
	Tau	Yod
		Nun
		Ayin
		Samech
		Tzaddi
		Qoph

The origin of the celebrated Kabbalist work, the *Sohar,* is obscure. One story tells of Simon ben Jochai (A.D. 70-110) who lived at the time of the destruction of the second Temple. Having been condemned to death by Titus, he escaped with his son and concealed himself in a cavern where he remained for twelve years. In this subterranean abode he occupied himself entirely with the contemplation of the sublime Kabbalah with the assistance of the Prophet Elias who visited him constantly and revealed some of the secrets which had been still concealed from the theosophical Rabbi. His son, R. Eliezer, and his secretary, R. Abba, as well as his disciples, subsequently collated Rabbi Simon ben Jochai's treatise, and out of these composed the celebrated work called *Sohar* or *Book of Splendour* or *Book of Brightness* which is the grand storehouse of Kabbalism.

The Kabbalah, as presented in the *Sohar,* depicts God as the En Soph, or Endless One and Boundless One. In his boundlessness, God cannot be comprehended by intellects nor described in words for there is nothing which can fully grasp and depict Him. Therefore, in order to make His existence perceptible and to render Himself comprehensible, the medium by which one interprets the En Soph consists of Ten Sephiroth or Intelligences, which emanate from the Boundless One.

The first Sephirah is called the Crown. The remaining Sephiroth are 2) Wisdom, 3) Intelligence, 4) Kindness, 5) Strength, 6) Beauty, 7) Force, 8) Splendour, 9) Foundation, and 10) Kingdom.

With regard to the Sephiroth, Christian Ginsburg suggests four things be kept in mind, namely: 1) the Sephiroth were not created by, but emanated from the En Soph; the difference between creation and emanation being, that in the former a diminution of strength takes place, while in the latter this is not the case; 2) the Sephiroth form among themselves, and with the En Soph, a strict unity, simply representing different aspects of one and the same being, just as the different manifestations of one and the same light; 3) since the Sephiroth simply differ from each other as the different colors of the same light, all the ten emanations alike partake of the perfections of the En Soph; and 4) as emanations from the Infinite, the Sephiroth are infinite and perfect like the En Soph, and yet constitute the first finite things. They are infinite and perfect when the En Soph imparts his fullness to them, and finite and imperfect when the fullness is withdrawn from them.

The Sephiroth which constitute the first Triad represent the intellect. Hence, this Triad is called the Intellectual World. The second Triad represents moral qualities and it is designated the Moral or Sensuous World. The third Triad represents power and stability and is called the Material World. These three aspects in which the En Soph manifests Himself are called the *faces*. The arrangement of this Trinity of Triads produce what one calls the Kabbalistic Tree or the Tree of Life.

The first Triad comprises the Crown, the head; Wisdom, the brains; and Intelligence, the knowledge, and is placed at the top of the diagram representing the heart or understanding. The second Triad comprises the two Sephiroth of Kindness and Strength, depicted by two arms of the Lord, one distributing life and the other death, plus the sixth Sephirah of Beauty which unites the two opposite Sephiroth of Kindness and Strength. The Third Triad comprises the two Sephiroth of Force and Splendour, designated the two legs of the Lord, plus the ninth Sephirah, Kingdom, representing the harmony of the whole Archetypal Man.

Three masculine Sephiroth are on the right, three feminine on the left and the four uniting Sephiroth occupy the center. The three Sephiroth on the right represent the principle of mercy and are called the Pillar of Mercy. The three on the left, representing the principle of rigor, are called the Pillar of

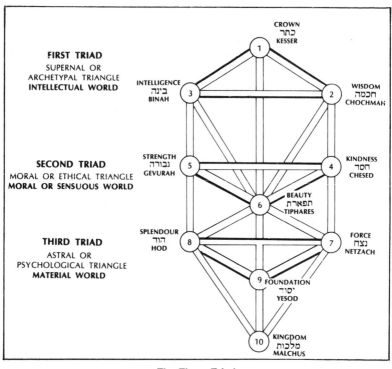

The Three Triads

Judgment. The four Sephiroth in the center, representing mildness, are called The Pillar of Mildness.

All the aspects of the Tree of Life are called paths. Each Sephiroth has a name as well as a number. The ten Sephiroth represent paths numbered from 1 to 10. The twenty-two connecting links between the ten Sephiroth are the *true* paths and they are numbered from 11 to 32. These twenty-two paths coincide with the twenty-two Major Arcana cards of the tarot deck. The sixteen court cards in the tarot pack correspond to the four levels known as the Four Worlds. The forty pip cards in the tarot pack, ten cards in each of the four suits, relate to each of the ten Sephiroth according to similarity of number.

Thus, The Tree of Life, depicted by Kabbalists as the manifestations of God expressed in the ten Sephiroth and the twenty-two connecting paths, correspond to the twenty-two Major Arcana cards of the tarot pack.

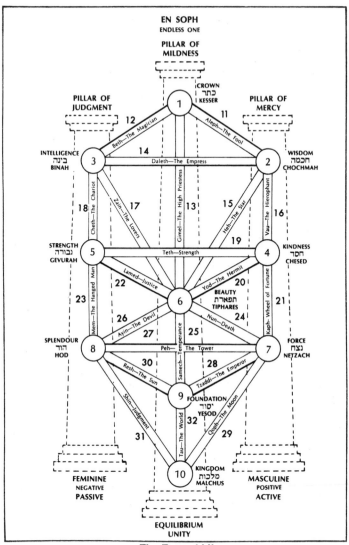

Within the diagram:

EN SOPH
ENDLESS ONE

PILLAR OF
MILDNESS

PILLAR OF
JUDGMENT

PILLAR OF
MERCY

CROWN
כתר
KESSER

1

12
Beth—The Magician

11
Aleph—The Fool

INTELLIGENCE
בינה
BINAH

3

14
Daleth—The Empress

2

WISDOM
חכמה
CHOCHMAH

18
Cheth—The Chariot

17
Zain—The Lovers

13
Gimel—The High Priestess

15
Heh—The Star

Vau—The Hierophant

16

STRENGTH
גבורה
GEVURAH

5

Teth—Strength

19

4

KINDNESS
חסד
CHESED

22
Lamed—Justice

Yod—The Hermit

20

BEAUTY
תפארת
TIPHARES

6

Kaph—Wheel of Fortune

21

23

Mem—The Hanged Man

26
Ayin—The Devil

27

25
Samech—Temperance

Nun—Death

24

SPLENDOUR
הוד
HOD

8

Peh—The Tower

7

FORCE
נצח
NETZACH

30
Resh—The Sun

28
Tzaddi—The Emperor

9

FOUNDATION
יסוד
YESOD

31
Shin—Judgment

Tau—The World

32

Qoph—The Moon

29

10

KINGDOM
מלכות
MALCHUS

FEMININE
NEGATIVE
PASSIVE

MASCULINE
POSITIVE
ACTIVE

EQUILIBRIUM
UNITY

The Tree of Life

The twenty-two paths of the Tree of Life are shown in numerical order in the following chart along with the appropriate Sephiroth, the letters of the Hebrew alphabet, the tarot symbols, and a description of the nature of the twenty-two paths as represented by the twenty-two emblematic tarot cards.

PATH	SEPHIROTH	HEBREW LETTER		TAROT SYMBOL
11	Chochmah (2) - Kesser (1)	Aleph	Ox	The Fool
12	Binah (3) - Kesser (1)	Beth	House	I The Magician
13	Tiphares (6) - Kesser (1)	Gimel	Camel	II The High Priestess
14	Binah (3) - Chochmah (2)	Daleth	Door	III The Empress
15	Tiphares (6) - Chochmah (2)	Heh	Window	XVII The Star
16	Chesed (4) - Chochmah (2)	Vau	Nail	V The Hierophant
17	Tiphares (6) - Binah (3)	Zain	Sword	VI The Lovers
18	Gevurah (5) - Binah (3)	Cheth	Fence	VII The Chariot
19	Gevurah (5) - Chesed (4)	Teth	Serpent	XI Strength
20	Tiphares (6) - Chesed (4)	Yod	Hand	VIIII The Hermit
21	Netzach (7) - Chesed (4)	Kaph	Palm of the Hand	X The Wheel of Fortune
22	Tiphares (6) - Gevurah (5)	Lamed	Ox-goad	VIII Justice
23	Hod (8) - Gevurah (5)	Mem	Water	XII The Hanged Man
24	Netzach (7) - Tiphares (6)	Nun	Fish	XIII Death
25	Yesod (9) - Tiphares (6)	Samech	Prop	XIIII Temperance
26	Hod (8) - Tiphares (6)	Ayin	Eye	XV The Devil
27	Hod (8) - Netzach (7)	Peh	Mouth	XVI The Tower
28	Yesod (9) - Netzach (7)	Tzaddi	Fish-hook	IIII The Emperor
29	Malchus (10) - Netzach (7)	Qoph	Back of the Head	XVIII The Moon
30	Yesod (9) - Hod (8)	Resh	Head	XVIIII The Sun
31	Malchus (10) - Hod (8)	Shin	Tooth	XX Judgment
32	Yesod (9) - Malchus (10)	Tau	Tau or Cross	XXI The World

PATH	BRIEF DESCRIPTION AND APPLICATION
11	From Wisdom to the Crown. Commencement. Frivolity. Levity. Innocence. Enthusiasm. Paradox.
12	From Intelligence to the Crown. Illusion. Manifestations. Skill. Craft. Subtlety. Spontaneity.
13	From Beauty to the Crown. Intuition. Understanding. Enlightenment. Knowledge. Education.
14	From Intelligence to Wisdom. Fertility. Fruitfulness. Attainment. Accomplishment.
15	From Beauty to Wisdom. Manifestation. Creation. Mixing. Opportunity. Optimism.
16	From Kindness to Wisdom. Spiritual. Kind. Humble. Compassionate. Merciful. Wise.
17	From Beauty to Intelligence. Faith. Love. Temptation. Testing. Perfection.
18	From Strength to Intelligence. Movement. Ordeal. Adversity. Effort. Action. Triumph.
19	From Strength to Kindness. Awareness. Reliance. Resolution. Spirit. Strength. Fortitude.
20	From Beauty to Kindness. Mediation. Prudence. Solicitude. Comfort. Wisdom. Counsel.
21	From Force to Kindness. Evolution. Change. Probability. Fortune. Destiny.
22	From Beauty to Strength. Moderation. Fairness. Justice. Satisfaction. Reward. Redemption.
23	From Splendour to Strength. Suspension. Transition. Renunciation. Abandonment. Sacrifice. Readjustment.
24	From Force to Beauty. Alteration. Change. Transformation. End and Beginning. Reincarnation.
25	From Foundation to Beauty. Moderation. Control. Accommodation. Temperance. Fusion. Combination.
26	From Splendour to Beauty. Test. Transfer. Subjection. Devil-worship. Weird. Astral. Magic.
27	From Splendour to Force. Breaking down. Unexpected. Undoing. Danger. Downfall. Ruin. Destruction.
28	From Foundation to Force. Proficiency. Skill. Leadership. Conviction. Domination. Realization.
29	From Kingdom to Force. Instinct. Pretense. Unknown. Distrust. Deception. Error. Scandal.
30	From Foundation to Splendour. Satisfaction. Contentment. Achievement. Pleasure. Reward.
31	From Kingdom to Splendour. Judgment. Spirit. Rejuvenation. Rebirth. Ascension.
32	From Foundation to Kingdom. Advancement. Completion. Facing reality. Success. Triumph. Perfection.

Arthur Edward Waite

Dr. Arthur Edward Waite (1857-1942) was a genuine scholar of occultism who painstakingly researched and wrote a number of works including *The Key to the Tarot* and *The Holy Kabbalah*. Waite utilized symbolism as the key to the tarot pack.

"The true tarot is symbolism; it speaks no other language and offers no other signs," wrote Waite. "Given the inward meaning of its emblems, they do become a kind of alphabet which is capable of indefinite combinations and makes true sense in all. On the highest plane it offers a key to the Mysteries, in a manner which is not arbitrary and has not been read in. But the wrong symbolical stories have been told concerning it, and the wrong history has been given in every published work which so far has dealt with the subject."

Under the initiative and supervision of Waite, a seventy-eight-card tarot pack known as the Rider deck was drawn by Miss Pamela Colman Smith, an American who had grown up in Jamaica and was a fellow member of the Order of The Golden Dawn.

Waite correctly surmised that The Fool, being unnumbered and representing 0, should not be placed between card numbers 20 and 21 as suggested by Levi and Papus, but instead its more natural sequence lay before The Magician in attribution to the first letter of the Hebrew alphabet, Aleph.

However, Waite also transposed, probably without adequate justification, the two cards of Strength and Justice. Strength, generally shown in tarot decks as number XI, is instead designated by Waite as number VIII. Justice, commonly shown as number VIII, is switched by Waite to number XI.

The attributions between the twenty-two Major Arcana cards and the Hebrew alphabet as represented by Levi and Papus in comparison to Waite are as follows:

HEBREW LETTER	LEVI AND PAPUS	WAITE
Aleph	I The Magician or Juggler	0 The Fool
Beth	II The Female Pope	I The Magician
Gimel	III The Empress	II The High Priestess
Daleth	IIII The Emperor	III The Empress
Heh	V The Pope	IIII The Emperor
Vau	VI Vice & Virtue or The Lovers	V The Hierophant
Zain	VII The Chariot	VI The Lovers
Cheth	VIII Justice	VII The Chariot
Teth	VIIII The Hermit	VIII Fortitude or Strength
Yod	X The Wheel of Fortune	VIIII The Hermit
Kaph	XI Strength	X The Wheel of Fortune
Lamed	XII The Hanged Man	XI Justice
Mem	XIII Death	XII The Hanged Man
Nun	XIIII Temperance	XIII Death
Samech	XV The Devil	XIIII Temperance
Ayin	XVI The Tower	XV The Devil
Peh	XVII The Star	XVI The Tower
Tzaddi	XVIII The Moon	XVII The Star
Qoph	XVIIII The Sun	XVIII The Moon
Resh	XX Judgment	XVIIII The Sun
Shin	0 The Fool	XX Judgment
Tau	XXI The Universe or The World	XXI The Universe or The World

"The Tarot embodies symbolical presentations of universal ideas," said Waite, "behind which lie all the implicits of the human mind, and it is in this sense that they contain secret doctrine, which is the realization by the few of truths embedded in the consciousness of all, though they have not passed into express recognition by ordinary men. The theory is that this doctrine has always existed—that is to say, has been excogitated in the consciousness of an elect minority; that it has been perpetuated in secrecy from one to another and has been recorded in secret literatures, like those of Alchemy and

THE FOOL .

THE MAGICIAN.

JUSTICE .

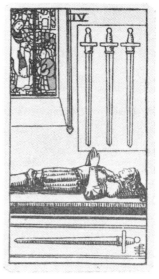

Waite Tarot Cards These are samples of the famous Rider pack created by Arthur Edward Waite and designed under his supervision by Pamela Colman Smith. The pack was first issued by Rider & Co. in London in 1910 and was recently reissued in authentic detail and true color tones by U. S. Games Systems, Inc., New York City. The pip cards bear a symbolic picture rather than only the suit symbol. Thus, the IV of Swords (Spades) depicts not only four swords but also a knight in the attitude of prayer at full length lying upon his tomb. The VI of Pentacles (Diamonds) depicts a young man in the guise of a merchant weighing money with a pair of scales while distributing money to the needy and destitute. The other four cards shown are from the Major Arcana and bear titles in English. The Fool pauses at the brink of a precipice above the great height of the world. The Magician with the eternal sign of life forming the figure 8 in a horizontal position above him raises his wand towards heaven while his left hand points to the earth. Strength depicts a woman closing the jaws of a lion. Justice reveals a seated woman balancing the scales of Justice in one hand and raising the double-edged sword in her other hand. The cards in this seventy-eight-card pack measure 2-3/4" x 4-3/4" and are round-cornered. The back design is a blue and black tarotée design.

Kabbalism; and behind the Secret Doctrine it is held that there is an experience or practice by which the Doctrine is justified."

The original Waite deck was published in 1910 by Rider & Company of London in conjunction with Waite's famous work: *The Key to the Tarot.* Several versions of the Waite deck in varying quality are available at most book and occult stores. In 1971 Rider & Company, in cooperation with U. S. Games Systems, Inc. of New York, reissued an authentic Waite-Smith deck known as the Rider pack and based upon the personal deck of Arthur Waite, still in the possession of his ninety-year-old daughter, Miss Sibyl Waite. This special tarot issue portrays the true images and colors of the original Waite deck and is the only authorized version.

Wirth - Case - Zain - Crowley

The twenty-two Major Arcana cards which accompany the book by Oswald Wirth, *Le Tarot des Imagiers du Moyen Age,* contain Hebrew letters depicted in the lower right corner of each card. For example, Aleph is assigned to card number I, *Le Bateleur* (The Magician). The Wirth cards are printed in striking metallic colors and are also Roman numbered at the top.

Paul Foster Case, in his book, *The Tarot, A Key to The Wisdom of the Ages,* uses designs for the twenty-two Major Arcana cards which in some instances are similar to the Waite designs. The Case cards bear an Arabic number in the lower left and a Hebrew letter in the lower right. For example, Aleph is assigned to The Fool while Beth is assigned to The Magician. The black and white line drawings of the Case cards readily lend themselves to coloring by an individual according to ones own personal taste.

The tarot pack used by C. C. Zain in his work, *The Sacred Tarot,* published by The Church of Light, is also black and white and suitable for coloring. While the cards are rich in Egyptian symbolism they are a complete departure from the usual tarot symbols.

The tarot pack presented by Aleister Crowley in *The Book of Thoth* is in full color based upon the original paintings by Lady Frieda Harris. These so-called "Thoth" cards are a complete departure from the usual tarot designs and were issued as a complete pack for the first time in 1971 for use with the book.

Other Tarot Decks

In addition to the customary twenty-two symbolic pictures on the Major Arcana cards used for fortune-telling, during the past two centuries various other designs have also appeared. These artistic decks were prepared as a pictorial presentation of the times and include such scenes as military events, art, science, literature, poetry, dancers, folklore, hunting, industry, comedy, etc. Especially prevalent in German tarots are scenes of animals. Although there are Italian, French, German, Belgian, Swiss and American tarots, the titles of the twenty-two emblematic designs are more frequently in French than in any other language, except for American tarot packs which, in the twentieth century, prevalently bear English titles. From the collector's standpoint these cards are especially colorful and interesting. They can be mounted with photo corners on large mat sheets thus avoiding damage to the cards while affording a colorful display.

Swiss Rochias Fils Tarot Cards This series of tarot cards dates from the late 18th century and was hand-stenciled at Neuchatel, Switzerland. The two of Coins states: *"Fait Par Jacque Rochias Fils à Neuchatel."* The High Priestess is metamorphosed into *La Papese*, the female Pope, while the grand Hierophant is depicted as *Le Pape*. Card No. XIII, frequently unnamed, appears with *"La Mort"*. Other cards shown: XVI *La Maison de Dieu*—The House of God or The Tower, and *Roi de Coupe*—King of Cups. The cards in this seventy-eight card pack are 2-3/8" x 4-11/16" and square-cornered. The backs are plain.

Carey French Revolution Tarot Cards The French Revolutionary tarot pack by L. Carey dates from (circa) 1791 and bears the distinction that the court cards are altered as follows: Kings-*Genie*, Queens-*Liberté*, Cavaliers-*Cavaliers*, Valets-*Egalité*. Additionally, the Empress and Emperor are demoted to *La Grand Mère* and *Le Grand Pere* and the crowns are removed as an outgrowth of anti-royalist sentiment. Judgment becomes *La Trompete*. The two of Cups is inscribed: *"Taros Fin de L. Carey à Strasbourg."* The cards in this seventy-eight-card pack measure 3-13/16" x 2-1/2" and are square-cornered. The backs are an alternating small sun and dot design in blue.

Tarot of Besançon Cards This seventy-eight card tarot pack dates from the early 1800s and is hand-colored using stencils. The two of Cups is inscribed in a space reserved at the lower end of the card: "RENAULT *Fabricant de Cartes (des Jouer?) à Besancon*." Renault apparently was the successor to J. Jerger, fabricator of tarot packs in the late 1700s at Besancon. *Le Charior* (The Chariot) bears the initials "J.I.A.B.", indicating J. Jerger at Besançon. Trump II, *Junon*, replaces *La Papesse* as is customary in most tarot packs from southern France. Other cards shown: III *L'Imperatris* (The Empress), VIIII *Le Capucin* (The Hermit), and *Cavallier de Baatons* (Cavalier of Batons). (Numerous misspellings are attributable to the illiteracy of the artisans who carved the woodblocks.) The cards measure 2-9/16 x 4-3/4" and are round-cornered. The backs are a mottled light red.

Polish Animal Tarot Cards This Polish Animal tarot deck in full color dates from the early 1800s and bears an inscription in the shield held by the Knight of Diamonds: *"Fabrique de Cartes de J. DuPort à Versovie"* (Warsaw). The paper wrapper bears Russian markings indicating the cards were probably made for use in Russia. The tax stamps on the Ace of Hearts are Polish. The designs on this pack are strikingly similar to and were probably taken from an earlier series of packs (late 1700s) by Andreas Benedictus Gobl of Munich, Germany. Also shown and unnamed are: The Fool, Trumps XII and XVI depicting animals in full length and the Queen of Spades. All trump cards are full-length except No. I which portrays a fanciful man with sword in hand. The full-color cards in the seventy-eight-card pack measure 2-3/16" x 4-1/4" and are square-cornered. The backs are a sun pattern inside open-ended squares in brownish-red.

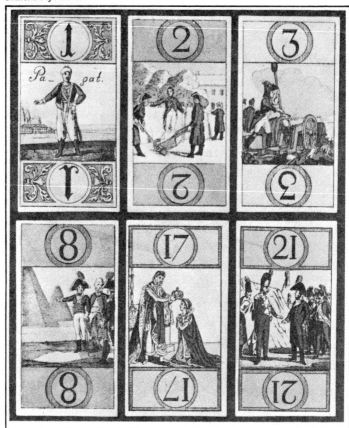

Napoleon Tarot Cards These rare Napoleonic tarot cards dating from (circa) 1812 are hand-stenciled in full color and depict important events in the life of Napoleon I. The trump cards bear double-ended Arabic numbers within a circle while the scenes are full-figured. Number 2 depicts the French military schools at Brienne-le Chateau where Napoleon was educated, while number 3 probably illustrates the seige of Toulon in 1793 with Napoleon commanding the French Republican artillery forces. Trump number 8 represents Napoleon either in Egypt in July 1798 at the time of the Battle of the Pyramids or in the following year when he defeated a Turkish force at Abukir. Number 17 depicts the crowning in 1804 of Empress Josephine by Napoleon at the time of his own "coronation" as Emperor by Pope Pius VII, and number 21 appears to be part of Napoleon's march into Germany. The meaning of trump number 1 is subject to conjecture. It is quite possible that the word *Pa-gat* stands for fortuitous leader, a prelude to the subsequent events in the life of Napoleon. The hand-stenciled cards measure 2-5/16'' x 4-5/16'' and are square-cornered. The backs are a multiple alternating design of squares and ornaments in grayish-blue.

Animal Tarot Cards Animal tarot cards from a seventy-eight-card pack probably made in Germany (circa) 1850. Each of the trump cards bears a double-ended number in Arabic. There are two double-ended animals on every trump card except number 1 which depicts the double figure of a boy. The Page of Spades and the Knight of Clubs are shown above. The full-color cards measure 2-5/16″ x 4-1/4″ and are square-cornered. The backs are a multiple dotted field of clumps joined by lines of several dots in blue.

Knepper Dance Tarot Cards These beautiful cards depict dance positions in full length. The pack totals fifty-four cards made by E. Knepper & Comp., Vienna in 1866 as evidenced by the tax stamp appearing on the Ace of Hearts (not shown). Shown in double-ended figures are the Cavalier of Clubs and Page of Diamonds. The cards measure 2-1/4'' x 4-1/8'' and are square-cornered. The backs are a multiple interlaced band with tiny circles and center squares in blue.

World War I Military Tarot Cards This fifty-four-card tarot pack, called *"Soldaten-Taroch"* was issued by Ferd. Piatnik & Sohne in Vienna. Designated card pack No. 217, the double-ended cards are lithographed on heavy stock. The pack omits the six through Ace in the suits of Spades and Clubs and five through ten of Hearts and Diamonds, as is customary with tarot cards in the game of tarock. The twenty-one trumps are numbered in Roman numerals and depict war scenes in full-length. The Fool is unnumbered. The court cards are anonymous soldiers and sailors except for the Queens which include a Red Cross nurse on the Queen of Hearts while the other suits depict young women working to aid the war effort. The cards illustrated left to right are: (*top*) VII Siege of Antwerp, XII Pilots over Venice, and XIII German U-Boat, Captain Konig, (*bottom*) XIX Liberation of Przemysl (Poland), XX The Overpowering of Citta Di Ferrara, and the court card, Page of Hearts.

Piatnik Tarock Playing Cards The Page of Clubs bears the name and address of the manufacturer Ferd. Piatnik & Sohne Wien. The II of trumps has the inscription *"Industrie und Gluck."* This colorful fifty-four-card tarot pack presents typical folk scenes double-ended on each card. This modern tarot pack, number 105A by Piatnik, measures 2-7/16" x 4-7/16". The cards are round-cornered and the backs depict a deer in the brush.

Muller Tarotrump Cards The above six cards are part of the
seventy-eight-card Tarotrump deck, produced by Muller & Cie of
Switzerland, now growing in popularity in the United States. The
game of Tarotrump is based upon the ancient games of Minchiate
and Tarocchi, slightly modified for today's playing-card enthusiast. The twenty-one Arabic numbered trump cards contain
double-ended folk scenes. The court cards bear the King, Queen,
Cavalier and Jack. The cards measure 2-5/16'' x 4-3/16''. They
are round-cornered and the backs have a blue tarotée or
crisscross design.

Grimaud Tarot Arista Cards Six of the seventy-eight-card Tarot Arista pack published by B.P. Grimaud of France. Each card bears a written description of the divinatory meaning and reverse meaning. Cards shown left to right are: (*top*) IX The Hermit with veiled lamp, XIV Temperance with two urns, and XX Judgment and the rising of the dead, (*bottom*) XXXVII King of Cups and master of the cup, LII Queen of Swords and mistress of the sword, and XL Page of Cups and slave of the cup. These card are unique because of the divinatory instructions presented on them which aids in fortune-telling. The cards measure 2-5/16'' x 4-1/2'' and are round-cornered. The backs bear a crisscross tarotée design.

1JJ Tarot Cards One of the most popular tarot packs in the United States is the 1JJ tarot fortune-telling deck comprising seventy-eight cards in full color. The six cards shown illustrate the fine artwork. *Le Mat* is The Fool. Card II follows the practice in southern France of using *Junon* instead of *La Papesse*. Card XIII is designated *La Mort*, Death. Card XVIIII *Le Soleil* represents the Sun. Two court cards are shown: *Roi des Epées*—King of Swords (Spades), and *Chevalier des Coupes*—Cavalier of Cups (Hearts). The cards measure 2-3/8'' x 4-3/8''. They are round-cornered and the backs have a black, green and brown tarotée design.

There are also popular today fifty-four-card and seventy-eight-card tarot packs used in the game of tarock. Another popular new game on the American scene, Tarotrump, is based upon the original rules of the 16th-century Italian games of Minchiate and Tarocchi slightly modified for today's playing card enthusiast.

The Tarotrump deck, illustrated on page 77, comprises seventy-eight cards:

56 cards in four suits of spades, clubs, hearts and diamonds. Each suit contains a King, Queen, Cavalier and Jack plus ten low or pip cards numbered 10 to 1.

21 Trump or emblematical cards numbered 21 to 1.

 1 Unnumbered card known as the Excuse.

78 Cards Total

The game of Tarotrump is for three to five players. In the three-handed version, twenty-four cards are dealt to each player and six cards form the stock. The stock subsequently becomes the property of the winning bidder.

Bidding begins with the dealer and there are four possible calls: I Pass! I Take! I Push! I Keep! The winning bidder, known as the Trumper, must have in his tricks at the end of the game sufficient points to equal or exceed his bidding obligation in order to win. The bidding obligation is determined by the number of Oudlers (Trump No. 21, 1 and The Excuse) in the Trumper's tricks at the end of the game.

If the Trumper holds in his trick pile:

3 Oudlers - must win 36 points
2 Oudlers - must win 41 points
1 Oudler - must win 51 points
No Oudlers - must win 56 points

Points are counted by the Trumper at the end of each game as follows:

Oudlers	Value
Trump No. 21	5 points
Trump No. 1	5 points
Unnumbered Excuse	5 points
4 Kings	5 points each
4 Queens	4 points each
4 Cavaliers	3 points each
4 Jacks	2 points each

When tabulating points, each of the above nineteen trump and court cards if held by the Trumper are counted with any of his remaining trump cards (numbers 20 to 2) or with any low cards (suit cards numbered 10 to 1) on a one for one card basis. The Trumper finally counts one point for each two cards remaining in his trick pile.

During the playing of the game, the leader of a suit may play any card and the other players, if possible, must follow suit. If unable to follow suit, a player must play trump (any of the trump cards numbered 21 to 1); if unable to follow suit or trump, a player may play any card.

The Excuse is a special card and may be played at any time. It *excuses* the player from his obligation of following suit or trumping. The Excuse remains the property of the player except if played on the last trick of the game when it is lost.

Trump No. 1 or the Little Trump, is the most delicate card in the pack. The player who holds the Little Trump and successfully makes the last trick of the game using the Little Trump receives a special bonus.

The complete rules and sample hands for the game of Tarotrump are available in the book, *Official Rules of the Tarotrump Card Game.*

✍ CHAPTER IV ✍

The Major Arcana Cards

THE TWENTY-TWO Major Arcana or emblematic cards in the Tarot Classic deck comprise twenty-one cards numbered from XXI to I plus an unnumbered card known as The Fool. The Major Arcana cards bear the following descriptive titles:

	The Fool	**XI**	Strength
I	The Magician	**XII**	The Hanged Man
II	The High Priestess	**XIII**	Death
III	The Empress	**XIIII**	Temperance
IIII	The Emperor	**XV**	The Devil
V	The Hierophant	**XVI**	The Tower
VI	The Lovers	**XVII**	The Star
VII	The Chariot	**XVIII**	The Moon
VIII	Justice	**XVIIII**	The Sun
VIIII	The Hermit	**XX**	Judgment
X	The Wheel of Fortune	**XXI**	The World

Following are descriptions of each card and its most significant Divinatory Meanings and Reverse Meanings as interpreted during several centuries of fortune-telling with the tarot pack. Persons reading the cards should bear in mind that the various meanings are suggestive and not meant to be conclusive. During a reading, the diviner of the cards should freely permit his own conscious and subconscious thought processes to assign expanded meanings to each card in a manner which feels most comfortable and responsive.

The Fool

(Unnumbered Card)

THE FOOL

DESCRIPTION:

A young man wearing a fools' cap and dressed in colorful garments wanders aimlessly, paying no heed to a dog barking at his feet. He is alone and unopposed. He wears a collar of pompons signifying frivolity. In his left hand, and resting over his right shoulder, he carries a stick symbolizing his desire and will. The stick is attached to a bundle bearing his previous experiences which he guards as a valuable possession for future use. The Fool has severed his prior dependency upon family and friends. His face expresses naivety and innocence. In his right hand, he loosely clasps a staff and, inattentive to details, he pays little attention to the direction in which he is walking. The bushes of opportunity spring up before him. The Fool is entering upon a new world of unlimited possibilities and self-expression. The sack carried by the Fool may also be emblematic of his faults which he refuses to accept, while the animal behind him represents his remorse pursuing him. The Fool personifies the spirit and enthusiasm of youth possessed by the boundless range of possibilities one perceives when setting forth upon a new undertaking. The Fool is a youthful and adventurous person.

DIVINATORY MEANING:

This card signifies folly. Thoughtlessness. Extravagance. Immaturity. Foolishness. Irrationality. Insecurity. Frivolity. Spontaneity. Pleasure. Levity. Lack of discipline. Inconsideration. Exhibitionism. Rashness. Frenzy. Unrestrained excess. Ridiculous expenditure or act. Carelessness in promises. Inattentiveness to important details. Beginning of an adventure. Infatuation. Indiscretion. Craze. Passion. Obsession. Mania. Tendency to start a project without carefully considering all the details. Initiative. Enthusiasm. Reluctance to listen to advice from other people. Tendency to be guided by self-intuition. The person drawing this card should be careful not to be tempted by that which appears better than it really is. Care must be taken to avoid foolishness and to make the right decision instead of taking the easy way out.

REVERSE MEANING:
Faulty choice or a bad decision. Indecision. Apathy. Halting or hesitating instead of proceeding diligently ahead. Lack of confidence.

I The Magician

DESCRIPTION:
A magician stands before a table on which various objects have been placed at random including knives symbolizing efforts and difficulties, coins signifying accomplishment and realiza-

tion of creative efforts, and cups signifying passions or good fortune. The double-ended phallic wand of creativity which he holds in his hand completes the four suits of the tarot deck of cards. The Magician's hat is shaped in the horizontal figure eight, the ancient occult number ascribed to Hermes and suggesting inner knowledge and the combining of the conscious and the subconscious into eternal and lasting fulfillment. His uplifted left hand draws power from above and, through the unity of his will and creativity of his ability, he brings things into manifestation through the down pointing right hand. This dual sign suggests that all things are derived from above to create all things on earth. The Magician is experiencing the establishments of his own identity through his own creativity and capabilities. He possesses the capability of employing the diverse objects on his table so as to succeed in thought, word and action. The Magician perceives life as a perpetual game of chance offering circumstances upon which some real control is realizable based upon individual capabilities.

DIVINATORY MEANING:

The Magician signifies originality and creativity. The ability to utilize one's capabilities in order to accomplish a task. Imagination. Self-reliance. Spontaneity. Skill. Willpower. Self-confidence. Dexterity. Ingenuity. Flexibility. Craft. Guile. Masterfulness. Self-control. Trickery. Misleading deception. Slight of hand. Bewilderment. Unity of thought and emotion. Ability to choose one's own actions. Determination to see a task through to completion. Capable of influencing other people.

REVERSE MEANING:

Weakness of will. Indecision. Ineptitude. Insecurity. Disquiet. Delay. Lack of imagination. The use of one's skills for destructive ends. Willpower applied to evil ends.

II The High Priestess

THE HIGH PRIESTESS

DESCRIPTION:

The High Priestess is seated within the precincts of her temple. She holds in her lap a book of knowledge and esoteric wisdom which records past events from both the conscious and subconscious mind. She is a large woman suggesting challenge to masculine supremacy. She is dressed in a long flowing costume with a great cloak tied at her neck and a sort of veil coming down from her two-tiered crown. She is the eternal feminine goddess of the ancient world bearing both knowledge and wisdom to the life around her. She embodies the perfect woman and the essence of all that is female but not particularly feminine in a romantic sense. She is sometimes called Isis, the ancient Egyptian goddess of fertility and sister and wife of Osiris. The High Priestess wears her crown to denote her stature in life. She is capable of absorbing and retaining significant amounts of diverse, factual details but finds it difficult to project this information into daily practical and meaningful application for herself. The High Priestess is the protector of this wisdom as well as the dispenser of knowledge to others. She is a teacher.

DIVINATORY MEANING:
Wisdom. Sound judgment. Serene knowledge. Sagacity. Common sense. Learning. Understanding. Serenity. Enlightenment. Objectivity. Penetration. Education. Ability to teach and instruct others. Foresight. Intuition. Comprehension. Perception. Self-reliance. Hidden emotion. Emotionlessness. Inability to share. Lack of patience. Uncomfortableness. Spinster. Platonic relationships. Tendency to avoid emotional entanglements. Occasionally talks too much. Sometimes too practical. A good teacher.

REVERSE MEANING:
Ignorance. Shortsightedness. Lack of understanding. Selfishness. Acceptance of superficial knowledge. Improper judgment. Shallowness. Conceit.

III The Empress

DESCRIPTION:

The Empress is depicted as a matronly woman seated upon her throne. She wears a crown on her head and stares ahead with resolution and stability. In her left hand she holds a scepter of authority while her right hand grasps a shield depicting an eagle, the symbol of her authority. She is represented with wings indicating the idea of spirituality. The Empress suggests the symbol of feminine productivity and action. She is resolute in appearance and determination. She is a woman of knowledge and intellect who can effectively put to use all her capabilities towards a meaningful and noteworthy development of her own life by means of a direct approach or subtlety if necessary.

DIVINATORY MEANING:

This card symbolizes feminine progress. Action. Development. Fruitfulness. Fertility. Attainment. Accomplishment. Interest in the day to day details of daily life. Mother. Sister. Wife. Marriage. Children. Feminine influence. Material wealth. Evolution. Sometimes subterfuge. Female guiles. Harassment. Spendthrift. Nagging. Capable of motivating others. A leader. Makes decisions founded upon all the facts at hand. The motivation behind a successful partner or husband. Business woman. Level-headed. Practical. Decisive. Intuitive.

REVERSE MEANING:

Vacillation. Inaction. Lack of interest. Lack of concentration. Indecision. Delay in accomplishment or progress. Anxiety. Frittering away of resources. Loss of material possessions. Infertility. Infidelity.

IIII The Emperor

A regal man of middle age with mustache and long flowing golden hair sits upon his throne surveying his domain. He wears an unpretentious crown because he does not need to make obvious announcement of his exalted position. He grasps outward in his right hand a ceremonial scepter indicating his active influence in all matters which come before him. He exudes confidence and accomplishment. His robes are ornamental and regal befitting his exalted position. Beneath his left hand is a shield with outstretched eagle, symbol of his authority, and suspended from a ceremonial ribbon around his neck is a circular golden amulet signifying his continuing power. He is placed against a background of open space indicating the scope of his dominion. The Emperor crosses his legs while sitting on his throne indicating in his relaxed position that he does not feel endangered and in his great capacity and responsibility he is at ease and able to perform the tasks that lie ahead.

DIVINATORY MEANING:

This card represents worldly power. Accomplishment. Confidence. Wealth. Stability. Authority. Indomitable spirit. Leadership. War-making tendencies. A go-getter. Paternity. Father. Brother. Husband. Male influence. Direct pressure. Conviction. Domination of intelligence and reason over emotion and passion. Strength. Patriarchal figure. Firmness. Attainment of goals. Desire to increase domination in every direction. Strong masculine development. Worthy of exercising authority. A capable person who is knowledgeable and competent. Willing to listen to counsel but then follows his own convictions.

REVERSE MEANING:

The reverse meaning of this card is immaturity. Ineffectiveness. Lack of strength. Indecision. Inability. Weak character. Feebleness. Failure to control petty emotions.

V The Hierophant

THE HIEROPHANT

DESCRIPTION:

An elderly man with heavy beard and mustache wears a
ceremonial miter on his head and in his right hand he clasps
the triple cross representing creative power throughout the
divine, intellectual and the physical worlds. Behind him are
two columns symbolizing on the one side law and on the other
side the right to obey or disobey thus the essence of being an

individual and deciding whether one shall live within or without the bounds of law. This is the theme of duality enabling man to choose mercy or severity and obedience through compulsion or freedom. The crown represents the material, formative, and creative worlds, repeating the symbolism in his staff. The Hierophant represents that which is orthodox and traditional even to the point of ineffectuality. The heritage and past symbols are often more important than the practicality and necessity of change needed in the present.

DIVINATORY MEANING:

Ritualism. Ceremonies. Mercy. Humilities. Kindness. Goodness. Forgiveness. Inspiration. Alliance. Compassion. Servitude. Inactivity. Lack of conviction. Timidity. Overt reserve. Captivity to one's own ideas. A person to whom one has recourse. Conformity. A religious or spiritual leader. At times this person is inept in adapting to new circumstances and changing conditions. Tendency to cling to former ideas and principles even if outdated. A person with a deep sense of historical importance and a sincere appreciation for past heritage.

REVERSE MEANING:

Overkindness. Foolish exercise of generosity. Susceptibility. Impotence. Vulnerability. Frailty. Unorthodoxy. Renunciation. Unconventionality.

VI The Lovers

DESCRIPTION:

A beardless youth without a hat stands beside a young maiden with golden hair. They both are depicted before a priest who faces them while they exchange their vows. Cupid's arrow points down on them. The Lovers represent all that is essential in the interaction of love and affection between human beings. This card design has obvious reference to marriage and friendship although some older versions suggest the symbols represent man standing between virtue and vice to which he must make a final choice. The overhead sun radiates its energy upon the creatures below and serves as a source of wisdom and creation. Cupid represents life beginning and the figures believe themselves to represent truth, honor and love to each other. This is a card of great sympathy, warmth, need and devotion and it offers an emotional experience with meaningful implications. But there is always the danger, in a romance so deep and beautiful, of possible trickery through blindness to reality and therefore caution is suggested.

DIVINATORY MEANING:

Love. Beauty. Perfection. Harmony. Unanimity. Trials overcome. Confidence. Trust. Honor. Beginning of a possible romance. Infatuation. Deep feeling. Tendency towards optimism. Oblivious to possible consequences. Letting oneself go. Freedom of emotion. The necessity of testing or subjecting to trial. Struggle between sacred and profane love. Putting to the proof. Examining. Speculating. Yearning. Tempting. Possible predicaments. A person deeply involved in the emotions and problems of a friend or relative. An affair of meaningful consequence.

REVERSE MEANING:

Failure to meet the test. Unreliability. Separation. Frustration in love and marriage. Interference by others. Fickleness. Untrustworthiness. Unwise plans.

ᏒᎧᎷᎧᏉ

VII The Chariot

DESCRIPTION:

A crowned conqueror stands erect in a cubical Chariot supported by four columns and covered with a luxurious canopy. He bears a scepter in his right hand and he wears a suit of armor with facial epaulets on each side. On his shoulders appear the faces of Urim and Thummim, seekers of the divine will of God through an oracular medium. The triumphal Chariot is drawn by two spirited horses representing the mixture of disturbance and distress and the union of positive and negative. The horses pulling in different directions compel the charioteer to control them. The Chariot represents the material currents which carry man along toward his destiny. The conqueror in his Chariot vanquishes those before him and he strikes out against all elementary forces to achieve victory. The horses are opposite in nature emphasizing that progress is achieved through attentive supervision of divergent details.

DIVINATORY MEANING:

This card suggests trouble and adversity, possibly already overcome. Conflicting influence. Turmoil. Vengeance. Success. Possible voyage or journey. Escape. Fleeing from reality. Rushing to decision. Riding the crest of success or popularity. Perplexity. Need for supervision. One must be attentive to details. Urgency to gain control of one's emotions. This card suggests that one can achieve greatness when physical and mental powers are maintained in balance and effectively put to work. Determination to mix hard work with times of productive solitude.

REVERSE MEANING:

The reverse meaning of this card is to be unsuccessful. Defeat. Failure. At the last minute to lose something otherwise within your grasp. Sudden collapse of plans. Conquered. Overwhelmed. Failure to face reality.

VIII Justice

DESCRIPTION:

The crowned female figure of Justice, depicting Astraea, Goddess of Justice in Greek mythology, is seated between the pillars of positive and negative forces. She is one of the cardinal virtues. Balanced in her left hand she holds the scales of Justice suggesting equitableness and fairness. In her right hand she grasps a double-edged sword, endowing her with the ability to decide right from wrong and indicating that sometimes action both ways successfully penetrates a difficult situation. Her face is resolute and firm in conviction. Justice is capable of the fair administration of manners and morals according to the best interests of the persons involved. She represents the pillars of moral strength and integrity. Although she wears no blindfold, Justice still remains fair and equitable. She does not permit temptation or envy to misguide her.

DIVINATORY MEANING:

Fairness. Reasonableness. Justice. Proper balance. Harmony. Equity. Righteousness. Virtue. Honor. Virginity. Just reward. Sincere desire. Good intentions. Well-meaning actions. Advice. Self-satisfaction. The eventual outcome, whether favorable or unfavorable, will truly be fair for the person concerned. Equilibrium. Poise. Impartiality. Capable of perceiving temptation and avoiding evil. This card suggests a person who responds favorably to the good nature of others. A considerate person. Someone who doesn't take unfair advantage of a situation.

REVERSE MEANING:

Bias. False accusations. Bigotry. Severity in judgment. Intolerance. Unfairness. Abuse.

VIIIl The Hermit

DESCRIPTION:

A bearded man in a voluminous habit holds upright in his right hand a lantern partially shrouded by his cloak. The lantern represents the knowledge of occult science. The Hermit walks with a staff in his left hand for support as he travels the path of initiation and knowledge. He is ready to come to the assistance of his fellowman with counsel and advice. The Hermit is the guardian of time. He is the wise man dispensing wisdom and truth from the eternity of knowledge which preceded him. He is the Ancient One in cowled robe whose comfort is the knowledge of the ages. His lamp of knowledge deals with all esoteric learning. Unfortunately, his knowledge, while complete, is often lifeless and impractical except in intellectual circles. At times his knowledge is so overwhelming that he carries it as a burden. His knowledge which should be utilized for advancement sometimes is a hinderance to the Hermit's creative thinking.

DIVINATORY MEANING:

Counsel. Knowledge. Solicitude. Prudence. Discretion. Caution. Vigilance. Circumspection. Self-denial. Withdrawal. Regression. Under certain circumstances this card also represents recession. Desertion. Annulment. Insincerity. Expressionless. A loner or person incapable of participating with another person. Misleading. Misguided. Tendency to withhold emotion. Fearful of discovery. Failure to face facts. Possessor of secrets which may or may not be revealed. Tendency to complacently dwell within this wealth of knowledge as something worthwhile without seeking to utilize the information towards some goal or application.

REVERSE MEANING:

Imprudence. Hastiness. Rashness. Prematurity. Foolish acts. Incorrect advice. Failure caused by result of dullness. Overprudence resulting in unnecessary delay. Immaturity.

X The Wheel of Fortune

THE WHEEL OF FORTUNE

DESCRIPTION:

The Wheel of Fortune contains six spokes indicating that each state of life is across the wheel from its opposite. Upon the wheel sit the crude images of a monkey descending on the left side, a tailed creature ascending on the right side, and a crowned sphinx with wings and tail resting at the top and holding a sword in its lion claws. The monkey on the left descending the wheel is falling into misfortune while the indeterminate figure on the right appears to be rising towards good fortune. These animals are depicted in the perpetual motion of a continuously changing universe and the flowing of human life while the sphinx sitting at the top seeks to maintain equilibrium. It is said that on the left the evil descending figure is Typhon, the monster in Greek mythology. The Wheel of Fortune revolves as a dispenser of sorrow and joy, life and death, good and evil, black and white, signifying that within all the elements of life there is a negative and positive. The Wheel is a circle without beginning or end and thus derives the symbol of perpetual eternity and continuous motion towards progress and change. The simultaneous ascent and descent suggests evolution and involution towards the destinies of fortune, chance, fate, probability, and predestined outcome. The sphinx at the top of the wheel indicates the principle of equilibrium and stability by which we have the power to alter our lives even though we travel the road of chance and fate.

DIVINATORY MEANING:
Destiny. Fortune. Fate. Outcome. Felicity. Godsend. Special gain or unusual loss. Culmination. Conclusion. Result. Approaching the end to a problem. The influences affecting the outcome of a problem. Good or bad depending upon influences of other nearby cards. Inevitability. Unexpected events may occur. The entire sequence of the Wheel suggests the course of things from beginning to end. Advancement for better or worse. Progress. That which was, is, and shall be remains the same unless one is alert to unexpected opportunity.

REVERSE MEANING:
Failure. Ill luck. Broken sequence. Unexpected bad fate. Interruption or inconsistency due to unexpected events. Outside influences not contemplated which adversely affects the spirit.

XI Strength

DESCRIPTION:

A woman courageously holds open the jaws of a lion-like creature which seeks to defy her. The creature appears stunned and the force required by the woman is minimal, evidencing the true inner strength that she possesses. The woman wears a large hat bearing the same horizontal eight that hovers over the head of the Magician indicating eternal and everlasting strength. The wide-brimmed hat also suggests the mixing of the conscious and subconscious minds resulting in the outcome of a strong person bearing great physical and mental strength. The lion or creature represents outside influential forces jeopardizing the woman and serving as a caution to the words and actions of others. The lion also represents temptations which may appear, requiring firm control and a resolute determination. This card of Strength, although a woman, represents all humanity and the accomplishments it can obtain through the strength of its convictions and tireless efforts.

DIVINATORY MEANING:

This card symbolizes strength. Courage. Fortitude. Conviction. Energy. Determination. Resolution. Defiance. Action. Awareness of temptation and the mental and physical abilities to overcome them. Confidence. Innate ability. Zeal. Fervor. Physical strength. Matter over mind, and, alternatively, mind over matter, depending upon the circumstances. Accomplishment. Attainment at considerable peril. Conquest. Hidden forces at work which are challenged. Heroism. Virility. Strength to endure in spite of all obstacles. Tireless efforts. Triumph of love over hate. Liberation.

REVERSE MEANING:

Weakness. Pettiness. Impotency. Sickness. Tyranny. Lack of faith. Abuse of power. Succumbing to temptation. Indifference.

XII The
Hanged Man

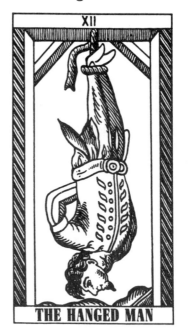

DESCRIPTION:

A young man hangs suspended from a wooden beam between
two pillars suggesting the shape of gallows. The structure may
also be a sort of gibbet, suggesting a warning. The man's feet
are tied with heavy cord and his hands are bound behind his
back. His left arm is bent at the elbow in the shape of a

triangle. His eyes are open and he remains fully aware and conscious of his surroundings. We see in the Hanged Man the moment of suspension at which truth and realization are revealed. The cloak of secrecy is removed. The inner self is exposed. Although the man is still earthbound he has attained in his fashion some measure of relief through the suspension and transition of his life. The young man teeters between the moments of decision. The events of the past are mesmerized in the present calm before the cascade of the future which lies in wait ahead. Repentance is the present salvation.

DIVINATORY MEANING:

Life in suspension. Transition. Change. Reversal of the mind and one's way of life. In a passive sense, apathy and dullness. Boredom. Abandonment. Renunciation. The changing of life's forces. The period of respite between significant events. Sacrifice. Repentance. Readjustment. Efforts may have to be undertaken to succeed towards a goal, which still may not be reached. Regeneration. Improvement. Rebirth. The approach of new life forces. This is the time to condition oneself towards new experiences. Surrender. Lack of progress. A pause in one's life. Outside factors having strong influence. You may sacrifice yourself too much. Your sacrifices may go unappreciated.

REVERSE MEANING:

Lack of sacrifice. Unwillingness to make the necessary effort. Failure to give of one's self. Preoccupation with the ego. False prophecy. Useless sacrifice.

XIII Death

DESCRIPTION:

A skeleton armed with a scythe clears the ground around him in which appear the heads and hands of victims. The skeleton lays waste to all life that appears around him. The Death card is the usual unlucky number thirteen with its foreboding of great change. Sometimes, the mowing down of the fields by the skeleton causes the springing up of new plants and the regeneration of former souls. The skeleton, which may be either male of female, represents changes of the present which will result in the events of the future. The energy of the skeleton serves as a breaking force to loosen the chains which bind and hold back change. The card of Death represents the transitional phenomena of decay and death modified to rebirth and reincarnation. The finality of the past is removed from the future through the irrevocable sweep of the scythe. The fear of change often overshadows the promise of new direction and the opportunities which await the person capable of altering the course of his life's direction. The reaper sweeps away the weeds symbolic of the confining conditions surrounding him, and the rebirth and regeneration begins almost immediately.

DIVINATORY MEANING:

A clearing of the way for new efforts. Transformation. Unexpected change. Loss. Failure. Alteration. Abrupt change of the old self though not necessarily physical death. The ending of a familiar situation or friendship. Loss of income or financial security. Beginning of a new era. Illness, possibly even death. Since great change may take place, this card, therefore, could mean a birth of new ideas or development of new expectations.

REVERSE MEANING:

Stagnatism. Immobility. Slow changes. Partial change. Inertia. Narrowly missing a serious accident or escaping from death or disaster.

XIIII Temperance

DESCRIPTION:

This card depicts the virtue of Temperance as a winged angel robed in golden garments and pouring liquid from one vessel to another vessel. Upon her shoulders rests thick flowing hair which falls in curls from her appealing face. The essence of life flows between the two vessels, symbolizing the flowing of the past through the present and into the future. The urns symbolize moderation and frugality. The pouring of the liquid from the higher urn held in the left hand to the lower urn clasped in the right hand—without spilling its contents—symbolizes great discipline and frugality. Behind the angel are hills and shrubbery indicating the unlimited opportunity which one can realize through successful combination of past and present events. The angel of Temperance possesses moderation and self-restraint. She is secure and self-reliant, capable of living within the modest needs of her position.

DIVINATORY MEANING:

Moderation. Temperance. Patience. That which can be accomplished through self-control and frugality. Accommodation. Harmony. The mixing or bringing together into perfect union. Management. Compatibility. Fusion. Adjustment. Good influence. Fortunate omen. Consolidation. Putting into successful combination. Ability to recognize and utilize the material and intellectual manifestations available to oneself. Possibly a person without excessive tendencies. Well-liked. Highly regarded. Mother image. Father image. Worldly image. Exuding confidence and complacity. Possibly too temperate and moderate to achieve a goal presently out of reach and requiring considerable aggressiveness.

REVERSE MEANING:

Discord. Disunion. Conflict of interest. Hostility. Inability to work with others. Difficulty in understanding others. Impatience. Sterility. Frustrations.

XV The Devil

DESCRIPTION:

This card shows a horned, bat-winged demon. holding a torch in his left hand and elevated on a pedestal. The Devil's right hand is upraised signifying black magic and destruction. Two horned and tailed figures are tied by their necks with thick cord to a ring bolt in the stone of the pedestal. The use of cord, instead of steel chain, suggests that, since we are subservient by our own failures, the bonds that bind us can be removed by us through determination and willpower. The Devil holds an extinguished torch, symbolizing destruction and evil intent. The Devil is the bearer of death, disaster and misery. This card indicates human suffering and desolation. The Devil personifies the person who is mischievous without regard to the effect upon others and the ultimate consequence. This card bespeaks of unfortunate circumstances and unhappy situations.

DIVINATORY MEANING:

Subordination. Ravage. Bondage. Malevolence. Subservience. Downfall. Lack of success. Weird experience. Bad outside influence or advice. Black magic. Unexpected failure. Seeming inability to realize one's goals. Dependence upon another person which leads to unhappiness. Violence. Shock. Fatality. Self-punishment. Temptation to evil. Self-destruction. Disaster. Astral influence. The tearing apart of one's self-expression to such an extent that the person becomes ineffectual. An ill-tempered person. Lack of humor except at another's expense. Lack of principles. Unethical.

REVERSE MEANING:

Release from bondage. Throwing off shackles. Respite. Divorce. Recognition of one's needs by another person. Overcoming insurmountable handicaps. The beginning of spiritual understanding. The first steps toward enlightenment. Overcoming the fear of one's own self.

XVI The Tower

DESCRIPTION:

A tall tower with crowned roof bearing four castellations is struck violently by a lightning flash, possibly originating directly from the sun. This card is variously called The Lightning Struck Tower, The House of God, The Hospital, Fire of Heaven or The Tower of Babel. Two persons, presumably a man and woman, fall to the ground along with falling drops of sparks and debris, symbolizing the descent of previous conditions and the breaking down of previous orders.

The Tower symbolizes previous knowledge and beliefs and sometimes false premises. It is made of bricks and has three windows, one over two, which indicate the limited view of the occupants. The Tower is struck so that just the top is severed from the main structure signifying a clean break from the past. The lightning is a symbol of strong and dominating occurance. The Tower represents a basic root substance from the past now undergoing destruction and change. The falling figures represent the headfirst leap away from the past and the plunge without recourse into the sphere of events which lie ahead.

DIVINATORY MEANING:

Change, in a complete and sudden manner. A breaking down of old beliefs. Abandonment of past relationships. Severing of a friendship. Changing of one's opinion. Unexpected events. Disruption. Adversity. Calamity. Misery. Deception. Bankruptcy. Termination. Havoc. Breakdown. Downfall. Undoing. Ruin. Divorce. Loss of stability. A sudden event which destroys trust. Loss of money. Loss of security. Loss of love and affection. Setback. Terrible change. Breakthrough into new areas.

REVERSE MEANING:

Continued oppression. Following old ways. Living in a rut. Inability to affect any worthwhile change. Entrapped in an unhappy situation. Imprisoned.

XVII The Star

DESCRIPTION:

A naked maiden kneeling on one knee by a pool pours the waters of life from two vases, signifying the stirring of new ideas and the precipitation of new concepts. The facial expression of the young maiden is one of satisfaction and hope. In the sky above hovers a huge star, the Star of the Magi, ablaze in gold, and surrounded by seven smaller stars which radiate upon the earth. The stars of hope ascend above the naked maiden. Birds and flowers are near at hand evidencing the birth of new life and promise. The bird is the sacred Ibis of thought while the stars represent the radiant cosmic energy. This card clearly represents the coming of new opportunity and the confidence of fulfillment. Water is the path of nonresistance and man has a choice to alter his way through new opportunity.

DIVINATORY MEANING:
This card depicts hope, faith, inspiration. Bright prospects. Mixing of the past and present. Promising opportunity. Optimism. Insight. Good omen. Spiritual love. Ascending star. Influence of the stars on your birth. Astrological influence. Culmination of knowledge and work from the past and present. Results which will soon come to pass from energies expended. Fulfillment. Satisfaction. Pleasure. The proper balancing of desire and work, hope and effort, love and expression. A favorable card suggesting that desire and energy are essential to happiness.

REVERSE MEANING:
Unfulfilled hopes. Disappointment. Pessimism. Bad luck. Lack of opportunity. Stubbornness. Bullheadedness. Imbalance. Conclusion of an unsatisfactory business experience or social friendship.

XVIII The Moon

DESCRIPTION:

Two dogs howl at the Moon from which drops of influence seem to be falling. The Moon has alternating gold and black rays signifying the conflict of good and evil influences. In the background, on either side of the dogs, appear two towers where man resides under the influence of the heavens. In the foreground, a crayfish hiding in a pool awaits the moment to crawl out upon its prey. This card suggests the presence in daily life of envy, deception, jealousy, prejudice, and it is a card of caution and danger. Moonlight is deceptive. The Moon demonstrates its power over the water and the crayfish lies in wait to deceive those who fail to heed the warning. There is a great deal of outside influence revealed in this card. Man is torn between many influences as he resides in his towers, influenced by the Moon's power, attracted by the dogs barking and ultimately tricked by the deceptive crayfish. The dogs have adapted to life with man but they remain a threat due to their susceptibility to the Moon's influence. This is a card of warning. This card indicates that events presently experienced may be obscured by future unexpected influences.

DIVINATORY MEANING:

Deception. Twilight. Obscurity. Trickery. Dishonesty. Disillusionment. Danger. Error. Caution. Warning. Bad influence. Ulterior motives. Insincerity. False friends. Selfishness. Deceit. Double dealing. Craftiness. False pretenses. Disgrace. Slander. Liable. Being taken advantage of. An insincere relationship. Superficiality. Unknown enemies. The meeting of many divergent influences. Falling into a trap. Being misled. Failure to avoid the dangers which surround. The chance of making an error is very great. The many different surrounding influences will combine into new pressures and impressions.

REVERSE MEANING:

A minor deception recognized before damage is done. Trifling mistakes. Overcoming bad temptations. Gain without paying the price. Taking advantage of someone.

XVIIII The Sun

DESCRIPTION:

A huge Sun complete with round face, flowing locks of hair and golden rays shines down upon two children wearing loincloths who embrace before a stone wall. The near nakedness of the children indicates they have nothing to hide from each other. The wall behind the children represents the efforts and past events which have taken place in a spiritual and physical sense and which are now attained and secure.

The children clasp each other signifying happiness and contentment. The Sun triumphs over them and its rays shine out and touch upon all the earth. From the Sun's rays flow strong and positive solar energies which permeate all living beings and give rise to feelings of contentment and satisfaction. The two children suggest the transformative rewards from the interaction between two people and the enlightenment and happiness which can result. This card represents the satisfaction of love and friendship and the contentment which results from love and devotion between two human beings. The day comes after night. The sun appears after the moon.

DIVINATORY MEANING:

Satisfaction. Accomplishment. Contentment. Success. Favorable relationships. Love. Joy. Devotion. Unselfish sentiment. Engagement. Favorable omen. A happy marriage. Pleasure in daily existence. Earthly happiness. The contentment derived from extending oneself to another human being. A good friend. High spirit. Warmth. Sincerity. The rewards of a new friend. Pleasures derived from simple things. Achievement in the arts. Liberation. Appreciation of small favors. Ability to accept life as it comes and to live contentedly.

REVERSE MEANING:

Unhappiness. Loneliness. Possibly a broken engagement or marriage. Cancelled plans. Triumph delayed although not necessarily completely lost. Clouded future. Lack of friendship.

XX Judgment

DESCRIPTION:

This card depicts a winged angel, possibly Gabriel, blowing a trumpet to which is attached a banner bearing the design of a cross. Below, a naked figure rises from a tomb while on each side a naked woman and man also rise with clasped hands. These figures suggest the rising of negative and positive life, the stirrings of the past towards Judgment and an evaluation of one's efforts and accomplishments. This card suggests not only the revival and reawakening of the individuals concerned but also a calling to atonement for that which is past and in the present, and a warning for what may lie ahead. The coffin may actually be the container of past wrongdoings now exposed for others to see and judge. We must live with our sins and one day we must account for our wrongdoings. The rising figures symbolize the cleansing away of the shroud of past times. The deeper our emotion the more significant our atonement. The greater our sorrow, the more meaningful our appreciation for joy.

DIVINATORY MEANING:

This card suggests atonement. Judgment. The need to repent and forgive. The moment to account for the manner in which we have used our opportunities. The possibility that present conduct towards other people is unfair and unkind. Rejuvenation. Rebirth. Improvement. Development. Promotion. The desire for immortality. The possibility exists that someone is taking unfair advantage of you and will be sorry in the future. Legal judgment in one's favor. The outcome of a lawsuit or personal conflict. One should carefully consider present actions as they affect other persons. Success will come easier if you are honest with yourself.

REVERSE MEANING:

Delay. Disappointment. Failure to face facts. Indecision. Divorce. Procrastination. Theft. Alienation of affection.

XXI The World

DESCRIPTION:

A nude female figure is encircled by a flowing veil or cloth while she stands in the center of a green, oval wreath, symbolizing the laurel wreath of victory. In each hand she holds a double-edged wand, symbolizing the power she commands from all sides. Though her legs form a cross, one foot is firmly placed on the ground and she is secure in her position. The two wands represent the powers resulting from all the efforts described in the preceding cards and the attainment of one's efforts through conscious and subconscious concentration. They also represent evolution and involution. In the four corners of the card are the four cherubic animals of the Apocalypse. To the upper left is a man or angel and to the upper right an eagle, both helping to support the wreath. Below the female figure are a lion and a bull, guardians of the truth. All that has taken place before now culminates in ultimate completion. The female figure is in command of her dominion. The four corners of the card also suggest the four elements of fire, water, earth, and air which are balanced to form the basis of life on earth and the composition of each day.

DIVINATORY MEANING:

Attainment. Completion. Perfection. Ultimate change. The end result of all efforts. Success. Assurance. Synthesis. Fulfillment. Capability. Triumph in undertakings. The rewards that come from hard work. The path of liberation. Eternal life. The final goal to which all other cards have led. Admiration of others. The outcome of events in spite of other signs. This is a very favorable card, especially if surrounded by other favorable cards.

REVERSE MEANING:

Imperfection. Failure to complete the task one starts. Lack of vision. Failure. Disappointment.

✿ CHAPTER V ✿

The Lesser Arcana Cards

THE LESSER OR Minor, Arcana cards of the Tarot Classic deck are divided into four suits containing fourteen cards each, corresponding to the suits in an ordinary deck of playing cards. There are the usual pip cards Ace to ten and the court cards King, Queen and Page (Jack) plus the Knight which is placed between the Queen and Jack.

The Kings in each instance wear large hats with the eternal symbol of the horizontal eight, whereas the Queens wear only crowns. The Queen of Pentacles and the Page of Wands are the only ones represented in profile. The personages depicted in the court cards generally hold the symbol of their suit, i.e. the King, Queen, Knight and Page of Swords each hold a sword. Careful examination reveals that the comparative similarities of pattern between the suits of Swords and Wands are distinguished from each other by the former being curved and the latter being straight. The four of Pentacles bears the initial "M" of the maker, Muller & Cie, and the two of Pentacles bears the design "Fabrique de Cartes à Schaff-

The Four, Three and Two of Pentacles

house." The Aces of Swords and Wands have the suit emanating from a cloud and firmly grasped by a hand.

The fifty-six Lesser Arcana cards, comprising fourteen cards in each suit, with suggested Divinatory Meanings and Reverse Meanings are as follows:

The Suit of Swords

(Correspond to Spades)

Swords generally represent courage, boldness, force, strength, authority, aggression and ambition. These cards represent activity, progress and accomplishment for good or bad, sometimes misfortune and disaster. This is the suit of leaders and warriors.

KING OF SWORDS

KING OF SWORDS

DESCRIPTION:

The King of Swords with long locks of curly hair sits on his throne resplendent in full armor. On his shoulders appear facial epaulets. The King represents power, authority, superiority, and the law. He holds upright in his right hand the sword of his authority and the sign (Sword) of his suit. His left hand rests upon his small unsheathed sword of confirming authority, available whenever he needs it.

DIVINATORY MEANING:

An active and determined person. Experienced. Authoritative. Controlled. Commanding. A professional man. Lawyer. Doctor. Engineer. Highly analytical. Justice. Force. Superiority. A person having many ideas, thoughts and designs.

REVERSE MEANING:

A person who may pursue a matter to ruin. Cruelty. Conflict. Selfishness. Sadism. A dangerous or wicked person. One who causes unnecessary disturbance and sadness. Perversity.

QUEEN OF SWORDS

DESCRIPTION:

The Queen of Swords is resplendent in beautiful robes. She rests upon her throne with upraised sword representing a quick-witted and capable person. Her left hand is raised as if to signify recognition or generosity. Her countenance is severe but chastened. She is one who has suffered a great loss and she bears up nobly under her misfortune.

DIVINATORY MEANING:

Sharp. Quick-witted. A keen person. Intensely perceptive. A subtle person. May signify a widow or woman of sadness. Mourning. Privation. Absence. Loneliness. Separation. One who has savoured great happiness but who presently knows the anxiety of misfortune and reversal.

REVERSE MEANING:

Narrow-mindedness. Maliciousness. Bigotry. Deceitfulness. Vengefulness. Prudishness. A treacherous enemy. An ill-tempered person.

KNIGHT OF SWORDS

KNIGHT OF SWORDS

DESCRIPTION:

The Knight of Swords dressed in regal armor sits upon his rearing horse and brandishes his sword. His left shoulder bears a facial epaulet. He is the defender of good and the opponent of evil. He symbolizes chivalry and bravery. He is good at heart and courageous. He is the forerunner of activity. His traits include a unique shrewdness which is not openly revealed. He is attentive and ready for any adversity or trouble.

DIVINATORY MEANING:

Bravery. Skill. Capacity. The strength and dash of a young man. Heroic action. Opposition and war. The headlong rush into the unknown without fear. The surrounding cards will indicate the influences around the Knight in his gallant pursuit. The Knight is a master in his art of action and warfare.

REVERSE MEANING:

Incapacity. Imprudence. Dispute or ruin over a woman. Impulsive mistakes. Conceited fool. Simplicity. Disunion.

PAGE OF SWORDS

PAGE OF SWORDS

DESCRIPTION:
A light-footed Page of Swords with fanciful hat and regal costume stands firmly on the ground with sword in his left hand. His right hand rests upon a stick, used for deception.

DIVINATORY MEANING:
This card symbolizes a person adept at perceiving, discerning and uncovering the unknown or that which is less than obvious. The quality of insight. Vigilance. Agility. Spying. A discreet person. An active youth. A lithe figure alert and awake to unknown dangers.

REVERSE MEANING:
Revealed as an imposter. Unforeseen. Illness is also possible. Powerlessness in the face of stronger forces. Lack of preparation.

TEN OF SWORDS

DIVINATORY MEANING: Ruin. Pain. Affliction. Sadness. Mental anguish. Desolation. Tears. Misfortune. Trouble. Disappointment. Grief. Sorrow.

REVERSE MEANING: Benefit. Profit. Temporary gain. Improvement. Passing success. Temporary favor. Momentary advantage.

NINE OF SWORDS

DIVINATORY MEANING: Misery. Concern. Quarrel. Unhappiness. Miscarriage. Anxiety over a loved one. Worry. Despair. Suffering.

REVERSE MEANING: Doubt. Suspicion. Slanderous gossip. Shame. Scruple. Timidity. Shady character. Reasonable fear.

EIGHT OF SWORDS

DIVINATORY MEANING: Crisis. Calamity. Conflict. Domination. Imprisonment. Turmoil. Bad news. Censure. Criticism. Sickness. Calumny.

REVERSE MEANING: Treachery in the past. Difficulty. Hard work. Depressed state of mind. Disquiet. Accident. Fatality.

SEVEN OF SWORDS

DIVINATORY MEANING: New plans. Wishes. Efforts through uncertainty. Attempt. Endeavor. Hope. Confidence. Fantasy. Design.

REVERSE MEANING: Arguments. Quarrels. Uncertain counsel or advice. Circumspection. Slander. Babbling.

SIX OF SWORDS

DIVINATORY MEANING: A trip or journey. Travel. Voyage. Route. Attempt through difficulties. Expedient manner. Success after anxiety.

REVERSE MEANING: Stalemate. Unwanted proposal. No immediate solution to present difficulties. Confession. Declaration.

FIVE OF SWORDS

DIVINATORY MEANING: Conquest. Defeat. Destruction of others. Degradation. Adversaries may arise. Revocation. Infamy. Dishonor.

REVERSE MEANING: Uncertain outlook. Chance of loss or defeat. Weakness. Possible misfortune befalling a friend. Seduction. Burial.

FOUR OF SWORDS

DIVINATORY MEANING: Respite. Rest after illness. Repose. Replenishment. Solitude. Exile. Retreat. Temporary seclusion. Abandonment.

REVERSE MEANING: Activity. Circumspection. Precaution. Economy. Guarded advancement. Desire to recover what is lost.

THREE OF SWORDS

DIVINATORY MEANING: Absence. Sorrow. Disappointment. Strife. Removal. Dispersion. Diversion. Opposition. Separation. Delay.

REVERSE MEANING: Distraction. Confusion. Disorder. Error. Mistake. Incompatibility. Separation. Mental anxieties. Loss. Alienation.

TWO OF SWORDS

DIVINATORY MEANING: Balanced force. Harmony. Firmness. Concord. Offsetting factors. Stalemate. Affection.

REVERSE MEANING: Duplicity. Falsehood. Misrepresentation. Disloyalty. Dishonor. Treachery. False friends. Lies.

ACE OF SWORDS

DESCRIPTION:

A hand appearing from a cloud holds a great sword which is encircled by the crown of authority. On either side of the sword grow branches and buds signifying progress and advancement. The card signifies the power of justice and the two-edged sword of equilibrium.

DIVINATORY MEANING:
Great determination. Strength. Force. Activity. Excessiveness. Triumph. Power. Success. Fertility. Prosperity. Deep emotional feeling. Love and vehemence. Championship. Conquest.

REVERSE MEANING:
Debacle. Tyranny. Disaster. Self-destruction. Violent temper. Embarrassment. Obstacle. Infertility. Hinderance.

The Suit of Wands

(Correspond to Clubs)

Wands generally represent enterprise and growth. Progress. Advancement. Animation. Invention. Energy. These cards also represent modest and humble persons. This is the suit of the laborer and worker.

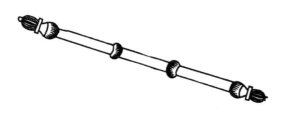

KING OF WANDS

DESCRIPTION:

The King of Wands bears a noble facial expression. He sits upon his throne wearing the crown of his authority and holding in his right hand the sign (Wand) of his suit. He is loyal and devoted. He radiates fatherly compassion and honest endeavors.

DIVINATORY MEANING:

This card denotes an honest and conscientious person. Mature. Wise. Devoted. Friendly. Sympathetic. Conscientious. Educated. A gentleman. Generally married. Fatherly.

REVERSE MEANING:

Severity. Austerity. Somewhat excessive and exaggerated ideas. Dogmatic. Deliberate.

QUEEN OF WANDS

DESCRIPTION:
The Queen of Wands is dressed in beautiful robes and holds a large scepter in her left hand. She rests upon her throne and wears a regal crown. Her long hair flows across her shoulders. She is a practical person with good common sense.

DIVINATORY MEANING:
A sympathetic and understanding person. Friendly. Loving. Honorable. Chaste. Practical. Full of feminine charm and grace. Capable of meaningful expression and love. Gracious hostess. Sincere interest in other persons.

REVERSE MEANING:
Jealousy. Deceit. Possible infidelity. Unstable emotions. Fickleness. Resistance. Obstacles. Opposition.

KNIGHT OF WANDS

KNIGHT OF WANDS

DESCRIPTION:

A handsome young Knight of Wands raises his menacing club, prepared for any adversity. He is anxious to meet the events of the future. His face shows no fear.

DIVINATORY MEANING:

Departure. A journey. Advancement into the unknown. Alteration. Flight. Absence. Change of residence.

REVERSE MEANING:

Discord. Interruption. Unexpected change. Quarreling. Breakup of personal relationships. Rupture. Discontinuance.

PAGE OF WANDS

PAGE OF WANDS

DESCRIPTION:

The Page of Wands stands in a pose of acquiescence. He clasps with both hands a large wand with severed branches. He may be a messenger or bearer of unusual news. He is a person with love for nature.

DIVINATORY MEANING:

A faithful and loyal person. An envoy. Emissary. Entrusted friend. A stranger with good intentions. A consistent person. A bearer of important news.

REVERSE MEANING:

Indecision in proceeding. Reluctance. Instability. Unable to make decisions. A gossip. Bearer of bad tidings. A person who may break your heart. Displeasure.

TEN OF WANDS

DIVINATORY MEANING: Overburdened. Excessive pressures. Problems soon to be resolved. Striving to meet a goal or to maintain a certain level or position. Possibly using power for selfish ends.

REVERSE MEANING: Difficulties. Intrigues. Duplicity. Treachery. A traitor. Deceiver. Subterfuge. Some losses will occur.

NINE OF WANDS

DIVINATORY MEANING: Expectation of difficulties and changes. Awaiting tribulation. Hidden enemies. Deception. Discipline. Order. A pause in a current struggle.

REVERSE MEANING: Obstacles. Adversity. Problems. Delays. Displeasure. Calamity. Disaster. Barriers to overcome. Ill health.

EIGHT OF WANDS

DIVINATORY MEANING: Swift activity. Sudden progress or movement. Speed. Hastily made decisions. Too rapid advancement.

REVERSE MEANING: Thorns of dispute. Jealousy. Harassment. Quarrels. Discord. Delay. Stagnation. Domestic quarrels.

SEVEN OF WANDS

DIVINATORY MEANING: Success. Gain. Overcoming obstacles and challenges. Surmounting overwhelming odds. Advantage. Victory.

REVERSE MEANING: Consternation. Anxiety. Embarrassment. Indecision. Hesitancy causing losses. Uncertainty. Perplexity. Doubt.

SIX OF WANDS

DIVINATORY MEANING: Conquest. Triumph. Good news. Gain. Advancement. Expectation. Desires realized. The results of efforts.

REVERSE MEANING: Indefinite delay. Fear. Apprehension. Disloyalty. Superficial benefit. Inconclusive gain.

FIVE OF WANDS

DIVINATORY MEANING: Unsatisfied desires. Struggle. Labor. Endeavors. Violent strife. Conflict. Obstacles.

REVERSE MEANING: Trickery. Contradictions. Complexity. Involvement. Caution against indecision.

FOUR OF WANDS

DIVINATORY MEANING: Romance. Society. Harmony. Newly acquired prosperity. Peace. Tranquility. The fruits of labor. Rest after peace.

REVERSE MEANING: Loss of full tranquility. Unfulfilled romance. Insecurity. Tarnished beauty. Incomplete happiness.

THREE OF WANDS

DIVINATORY MEANING: Practical knowledge. Business acumen.

Strength. Enterprise. Negotiations. Trade. Commerce. Undertaking.

REVERSE MEANING: Assistance with an ulterior motive. Treachery. Cessation of adversity. Beware of help offered.

TWO OF WANDS

DIVINATORY MEANING: Mature individual. Ruler. Attainment of goals and needs. Boldness. Courage in undertakings. A dominant personality.

REVERSE MEANING: Sadness. Trouble. Restraint caused by others. Loss of faith. Unexpected surprise.

ACE OF WANDS

DESCRIPTION:

The hand of Life appears from a cloud. It holds a large wand from which fall many leaves and flowers signifying fertility and progress and the descent of life towards eventual rejuvenation and rebirth.

DIVINATORY MEANING:
Creation. Beginning. Invention. Start of an undertaking. Fortune. Enterprise. Gain. Inheritance. Birth of a child. Beginning of a meaningful experience. An adventure. Escapade.

REVERSE MEANING:
False start. Cloudy outlook. Unrealized goal. Decadence. Empty existence. Vexation. Cancellation of plans.

The Suit of Cups

(Correspond to Hearts)

Cups generally represent love, happiness, gaiety and joy. The cups hold water which is a symbol of pleasure and happiness. These cards represent passions and deep feeling. This is the suit of the humane person.

KING OF CUPS

KING OF CUPS

DESCRIPTION:

The King of Cups, wearing a thick beard and mustache, clasps a great cup in his right hand and rests the base of the cup upon his knee. He wears a regal crown and his vestments are rich and majestic. He is levelheaded and responsible. The King personifies a kind and considerate person who is peaceful and interested in the arts.

DIVINATORY MEANING:

Responsibility and creativity. Learned person. Professional. Businessman. Lawyer. Artist. Religious person. Scientist. A considerate person. Kindly. Reliable. Responsible. Liberal in manner. Interested in the arts and sciences. Generous.

REVERSE MEANING:

Artistic temperament. Double-dealing. Dishonesty. Scandal. Loss. Ruin. Injustice. A crafty person without virtue. Shifty in dealings.

QUEEN OF CUPS

DESCRIPTION:

The Queen of Cups holds a great cup in her right hand. She is robed in rich and majestic vestments. She personifies a loving, devoted and practical person. She is capable of putting into practice her dreams and visions.

DIVINATORY MEANING:

A warm-hearted and fair person. Poetic. Beloved. Adored. Good friend and mother. Devoted wife. Practical. Honest. Possesses loving intelligence. Gift of vision.

REVERSE MEANING:

Inconsistency of honor. Possible immorality. Dishonesty. Unreliability. Vice. Not to be trusted.

KNIGHT OF CUPS

KNIGHT OF CUPS

DESCRIPTION:

The Knight of Cups rides gracefully on his horse. He balances a great cup in his right hand and appears contemplative. He is approaching his destiny. He dreams the highest of aspirations.

DIVINATORY MEANING:

An invitation or opportunity may soon arise. Arrival. Approach. Advancement. Attraction. Inducement. Appeal. Request. Challenge. Proposal. Proposition.

REVERSE MEANING:

Subtlety. Artifice. Trickery. Deception. Fraud. A sly and cunning person. A person cabable of swindling.

PAGE OF CUPS

PAGE OF CUPS

DESCRIPTION:
A somewhat studious and serious Page of Cups holds in his right hand a great cup upraised before him. He is a loyal and helpful person. In his left hand he clutches his hat, symbol of obediance.

DIVINATORY MEANING:
A studious and intent person. Reflective. Meditative. Loyal. Willing to offer services and efforts towards a specific goal. A helpful person. A trustworthy worker.

REVERSE MEANING:
Inclination. Deviation. Susceptibility. Temporary distraction. Seduction. A flatterer.

TEN OF CUPS

DIVINATORY MEANING: Home. Abode. Happiness. Joy. Pleasure. Peace. Love. Contentment. Good family life. Honor. Esteem. Virtue. Reputation.

REVERSE MEANING: Loss of friendship. Unhappiness. Family quarrel. Pettiness. Rage. Combat. Strife. Opposition. Differences of opinion.

NINE OF CUPS

DIVINATORY MEANING: Success. Material attainment. Advantage. Well-being. Abundance. Good health. Victory. Difficulties surmounted.

REVERSE MEANING: Mistakes. Material loss. Imperfections. Misplaced truth. False freedom. Opposition. Differences. Dispute.

EIGHT OF CUPS

DIVINATORY MEANING: Discontinuance of effort. Disappointment. Abandonment of previous plans. Shyness. Modesty. Abandoned success.

REVERSE MEANING: Happiness. Effort continued until full success is attained. Festivity. Joy. Gaiety. Feasting.

SEVEN OF CUPS

DIVINATORY MEANING: Fantasy. Unrealistic attitudes. Imagination. Daydreams. Foolish whims. Wishful thinking. Illusionary success.

REVERSE MEANING: Desire. Determination. Strong willpower. A goal nearly attained. Intelligent choice. Desire. Will. Resolution.

SIX OF CUPS

DIVINATORY MEANING: Memories. Past influences. Things that have vanished. Childhood passed. Nostalgia. Faded images. Longing.

REVERSE MEANING: The future. Opportunities ahead. Coming events. New vistas. Plans that may fail. That which will shortly arrive.

FIVE OF CUPS

DIVINATORY MEANING: Partial loss. Regret. Friendship without real meaning. Marriage without real love. Imperfection. Flaw. Inheritance. Incomplete union or partnership.

REVERSE MEANING: Hopeful outlook. Favorable expectations. New alliances. Affinity. Return of an old friend. Reunion.

FOUR OF CUPS

DIVINATORY MEANING: Weariness. Aversion. Disgust. Disappointment. Unhappiness. Bitter experience. Stationary period in one's life.

REVERSE MEANING: New possibilities. New relationships. New approaches to old problems. New acquaintance. New knowledge.

THREE OF CUPS

DIVINATORY MEANING: Resolution of a problem. Conclusion. Solace. Healing. Satisfactory result. Fulfillment. Compromise.

REVERSE MEANING: Excessive pleasures. Overabundance. Superfluity. Loss of prestige. Delays. Unappreciation.

TWO OF CUPS

DIVINATORY MEANING: Love. Friendship beginning or renewed. Passion. Union. Engagement. Understanding. Cooperation. Partnership. Marriage.

REVERSE MEANING: Unsatisfactory love. False friendship. Troubled relationship. Divorce. Separation. Crossed desires. Opposition. Disunion. Misunderstanding.

ACE OF CUPS

DESCRIPTION:

A large ornate cup signifies the holding of great abundance.

Near the cup rise branches and flowers symbolizing regeneration and growth.

DIVINATORY MEANING:
Great abundance. Fulfillment. Perfection. Joy. Fertility. Opulence. Fullness. Happiness. Productiveness. Beauty and pleasure. Goodness overflowing. Favorable outlook.

REVERSE MEANING:
Change. Alteration. Erosion. Instability. Sterility. Unrequited love. Clouded joy. False heart. Inconsistency.

The Suit of Pentacles

(Correspond to Diamonds)

Pentacles generally represent material and financial matters. This may take the form of money, occupation, material gain, business development, etc. These cards represent deep sensitivity and involvement. This is the suit of the merchant and tradesman.

KING OF PENTACLES

KING OF PENTACLES

DESCRIPTION:

The King of Pentacles sits upon his throne displaying a great coin, the sign of his suit. His expression is that of an experienced, capable and prosperous person. He is dressed in rich blue robes and he wears a wide brimmed figure-eight hat. His legs are crossed, suggesting his confidence and ability.

DIVINATORY MEANING:

An experienced and successful leader. A person of character and intelligence. Business acumen. Mathematical ability. Loyal friend. Reliable in marriage. Successful businessman. Wise investments. Affinity to acquire money and valuable possessions.

REVERSE MEANING:

Corruption. Using any means to achieve the desired end. Vice. Avarice. Unfaithfulness. An old and vicious man. Peril. Danger. Thriftless.

QUEEN OF PENTACLES

DESCRIPTION:

The Queen of Pentacles holds aloft the great coin of her suit. Her face expresses intelligence, awareness and generosity. In her left hand she holds a treasured ornament on a golden scepter. She stands before her throne in full view of her subjects.

DIVINATORY MEANING:

Prosperity and well-being. Wealth. Abundance. Luxury. Opulence. Extreme comfort. Generosity. Security. Liberty. Magnificence. Grace. Dignity. A rich person but generous and charitable. A noble soul.

REVERSE MEANING:

False prosperity. Suspense. Suspicion. Responsibilities neglected. Vicious person. Untrusting person. Fearful of failure.

KNIGHT OF PENTACLES

KNIGHT OF PENTACLES

DESCRIPTION:

The Knight of Pentacles sits majestically upon his horse with the great coin of his suit behind him in the heavens. Both the Knight and his horse express confidence and accomplishment. The Knight is a materialist. He is capable of succeeding at most goals.

DIVINATORY MEANING:

A mature and responsible person. Reliable. Methodical. Patient. Persistent. Ability to conclude a task. Laborious. Organized. Capable. A dependable person.

REVERSE MEANING:

Stagnation. Carelessness. Inertia. Lack of determination or direction. Narrow-mindedness. Limited by dogmatic views. Idleness.

PAGE OF PENTACLES

DESCRIPTION:

An articulate Page of Pentacles holds the great coin in his left hand before him. He stares fixedly ahead as if dreaming and unaware of that which is about him. Below him rests another coin while bushes spring up nearby signifying abundance.

DIVINATORY MEANING:

Deep concentration and application. Study. Scholarship. Reflection. Respect for knowledge. Desire for learning and new ideas. A do-gooder. Bearer of news.

REVERSE MEANING:

An unrealistic person. Failure to recognize obvious facts. Dissipation of ideas. Illogical thinking. Rebelliousness. Wastefulness. Loss. Unfavorable news.

TEN OF PENTACLES

DIVINATORY MEANING: Prosperity. Riches. Security. Safety. Family. Ancestry. Inheritance. Family matters. Home. Dwelling.

REVERSE MEANING: Poor risk. Bad odds. Possible loss. Hazard. Robbery. Loss of inheritance. Dissipation. Gambling.

NINE OF PENTACLES

DIVINATORY MEANING: Accomplishment. Discernment. Discretion. Foresight. Safety. Prudence. Material well-being. Love of nature.

REVERSE MEANING: Threat to safety. Roguery. Dissipation. Danger. Storms. Bad faith. Possible loss of a valued friendship or a treasured possession.

EIGHT OF PENTACLES

DIVINATORY MEANING: Apprenticeship. Craftsmanship. Fast to learn. Candor. Frankness. Modesty. Handiwork. Personal effort.

REVERSE MEANING: Lack of ambition. Vanity. Conceit. Disillusionment. Usury. Hypocrisy. Flattery. Intrigue.

SEVEN OF PENTACLES

DIVINATORY MEANING: Ingenuity. Growth. Hard work. Progress. Successful dealings. Money. Wealth. Treasure. Gain.

REVERSE MEANING: Anxiety. Impatience. Uneasiness. Imprudent actions. Loss of money. Unwise investments.

SIX OF PENTACLES

DIVINATORY MEANING: Generosity. Philanthropy. Charity. Kindness. Gratification. Gifts. Material gain.

REVERSE MEANING: Avarice. Selfishness. Envy. Jealousy. Ungiving of one's self. Bad debts. Unpaid loans.

FIVE OF PENTACLES

DIVINATORY MEANING: Material trouble. Destitution. Loss. Failure. Error. Impoverishment. Mistress. Lover. Affection.

REVERSE MEANING: Reversal of bad trend. New interest in matters. Overcoming ruin. Disharmony in marriage or love interests.

FOUR OF PENTACLES

DIVINATORY MEANING: Love of material wealth. Hoarder. Usurer. Skinflint. Miser. Ungenerous person. Inability to share.

REVERSE MEANING: Setbacks in material holdings. Obstacles. Opposition to further gain. Suspense and delay. Spendthrift.

THREE OF PENTACLES

DIVINATORY MEANING: Great skill in trade or work. Mastery. Perfection. Artistic ability. Dignity. Renown. Rank. Power.

REVERSE MEANING: Sloppiness. Mediocrity. Lower quality. Money problems. Commonplace ideas. Lack of skill. Preoccupation.

TWO OF PENTACLES

DIVINATORY MEANING: Difficulty in launching new projects. Difficult situations arising. New troubles. Embarrassment. Worry. Concern.

REVERSE MEANING: Literary ability. Agility in handling matters. Simulated enjoyment. Enforced gaiety. Letter. Message. Missive.

ACE OF PENTACLES

DESCRIPTION:
A large coin signifies very favorable outlook and prosperity. This card symbolizes the realization of counterbalanced ideas.

DIVINATORY MEANING:
Perfection. Attainment. Prosperity. Felicity. Great wealth.

Riches. Bliss. Ecstasy. Gold. Valuable coins or artifacts. Treasures. The combination of material and spiritual prosperity.

REVERSE MEANING:

Prosperity without happiness. Misused wealth. Wasted money. Corruption by money. Miserliness. Greed. Fool's gold.

c✍ CHAPTER VI ✍ɔ

Spreading The Major Arcana

THE PRACTICAL APPLICATIONS of the tarot pack occur
during the shuffling, spreading and interpretation of the cards.
Some persons are undoubtedly born with the gift of pre-
monition and intuition. Other persons develop a sixth sense or
knack for prediction. The allegorical cards of the tarot pack
stimulate the mind and reveal a story based upon the meaning
of each card as interpreted by the responsiveness of the diviner
or interpreter.

Fatalists, believing that the course of events is pre-
determined and that we pursue our daily activities following a
predestined pattern, are generally more favorably disposed
towards fortune-telling and clairvoyance because of their
acceptance of the existence of pre-established life patterns.

However, it is also recognized that cartomancy awakens the
mind to the existence of future possibilities which may

otherwise have been overlooked. A person proceeding in a given established pattern may significantly modify the final outcome through the realization of new found opportunities subsequently achieved through greater efforts. Thus, we are in fact *qualified* masters of our fate, capable of modifying our own destiny within certain limits.

There are numerous methods of spreading the tarot cards and some of them are exceedingly complicated and cumbersome. One of the earliest and most effective spreads, the ten-card spread, utilizes only the twenty-two Major Arcana cards, although the entire deck may also be employed (see Chapter VII). After several practice spreadings and interpretations this method will become quite natural and easy to use.

The fifty-six Lesser Arcana cards are set aside. The diviner, also known as the reader or interpreter, places the Major Arcana cards in numerical sequence from I to XXI. The unnumbered card entitled The Fool is placed either at the beginning of the deck, in the middle of the deck, between the twentieth and twenty-first numbered cards or at the very end of the deck. Generally, The Fool is best placed at the very beginning of the deck, in front of The Magician, and facing out. Arrange the pack in order so that, upon placing the twenty-two-card pack face down on the table, The Fool is face down and closest to the table.

The person seeking an answer to a question, or wishing a general reading of the past, present and future in terms of current perspective, is known as the questioner or querent. The questioner sits at a table opposite the diviner. Both persons should maintain a serious mental attitude. There should be no disturbing outside or surrounding influences such as cross conversation or glaring lights. The questioner must put all other thoughts and desires from his mind except the specific or general question which he states aloud to the diviner while simultaneously shuffling the cards face down.

The person who shuffles the cards impregnates them with his own personal magnetism and thereby creates a rapport between the conscious and subconscious states of his mind and the cards. The cards may be shuffled either hand over hand or by riffling (separating the deck into two parts and riffling with the thumb so the cards intermix). The shuffling *must* be done by the person who wishes to have an interpretation or prediction concerning himself or an answer to his question, and not by the diviner, reader or interpreter. The sequence of cards, both consciously or subconsciously, is set by the manner of the shuffling as determined by the questioner *without looking at the cards*. Thus, the questioner has an unpredetermined yet obvious and direct influence over the cards used in the final spread and reading.

When the questioner is satisfied with his shuffling, he places the deck face down on the table in front of the diviner. It is usually better to use a table of dark color for divination rather than, for example, a white kitchen table or counter, which may distract the diviner. The cards are always viewed from the diviner's position. Beginning with the top face down card as number one, the second card as number two, and so on, the diviner turns up the first six cards and places them face up on the table in the sequence shown in the diagram on page 167.

The diviner should turn the cards over from left to right thereby assuring that the cards continue to point in the same direction as placed on the table by the questioner. The cards which face the diviner are said to be positioned for a strong, positive reading and the cards which face the questioner are said to be upside down or inverted. Therefore, they have a weak, delayed or even reversed meaning. In the event the first card turned over by the diviner is reversed or upside down, the diviner should reverse the first card so that it is upright and

turn over the remaining nine cards from the bottom to the top
in such a manner as to reverse the direction of each of the cards
since, inadvertently, the questioner may have placed the entire
pack upside down before the diviner.

The correct manner of turning over the cards is illustrated in
the following diagram:

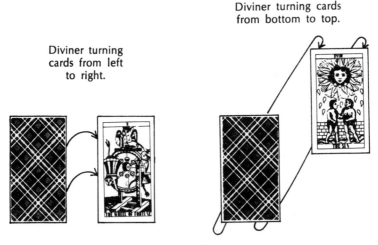

Diviner turning cards
from bottom to top.

Diviner turning
cards from left
to right.

Turning the Cards

Generally, if more than half of the cards are reversed, the
diviner may realize a more consistent and meaningful reading
by returning all the reversed cards to their upright position.

The sequence of laying out the cards in the ten-card spread
is as follows:

CARD NUMBER 1—Present Position: Atmosphere in which
the questioner is presently working and living. Shows the area
of influence in which the questioner presently exists and the
atmosphere in which the other currents are working. This card
represents the questioner.

CARD NUMBER 2—Immediate Influence: Shows the nature of the influence or immediate sphere of involvement or obstacles which lie just ahead. This card crosses the questioner.

CARD NUMBER 3—Goal or Destiny: Shows the ultimate goal or destiny of the questioner. Indicates the best that can be accomplished by the questioner based upon the existing circumstances. This card also may represent the questioner's aim or ideal in the matter within his present frame of reference. This card crowns the questioner.

CARD NUMBER 4—Distant Past Foundation: Shows the broad and basic events and influences which existed in the past and upon which the present events are taking place. It is the basis of fact already passed into actuality and which is embodied within the questioner. This card is placed beneath the questioner.

CARD NUMBER 5—Recent Past Events: Shows the most recent sphere of influence or events which have just passed or which are just passing. This card may also represent distant past influences exerting recent past influences of an inordinately strong nature. This card is behind the questioner.

CARD NUMBER 6—Future Influence: Shows the sphere of influence that is coming into being in the near future in a broad sense. This card is before the questioner.

After the diviner has read the above six cards, he then proceeds to turn over the next four cards from the deck, placing them one above the other in a line, to the right of the previous six cards, as shown in the diagram.

CARD NUMBER 7—The Questioner: Shows the questioner in his present position or attitude within the circumstances surrounding him. Attempts to place the questioner in proper perspective.

Card
No. 10
Final
Result

Card
No. 3
Goal
or
Destiny

Card
No. 9
Inner
Emotions

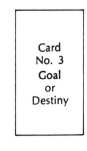

Card No. 1
Present
Position

Card No. 2
Immediate
Influence

Card
No. 4
Distant
Past
Founda-
tion

Card
No. 6
Future
Influence

Card
No. 8
Environ-
mental
Factors

Card
No. 5
Recent
Past
Events

Card
No. 7
The
Question-
er

CARD NUMBER 8—Environmental Factors: Shows the questioner's influence on other people and his position in life. Reveals those tendencies and factors which exist with respect to other persons which may have an effect on the questioner.

CARD NUMBER 9—Inner Emotions: Shows the inner hopes, fears, anxieties and hidden emotions of the questioner, including those thoughts that will come to the mind of the questioner in the future. This card may also reveal secrets which the questioner keeps from other people and ulterior motives which concern the questioner.

CARD NUMBER 10—Final Result: Shows the culmination and result which will be brought about from all of the influences as revealed by the other cards in the divination provided events and influences continue as indicated.

After reading each individual card the diviner should go back and interpret the cards as they relate to each other. For example, Card Number 4—Distant Past Foundation, may show a similarity to Card Number 5—Recent Past Events. Likewise, a striking connection may exist between Card Number 1—Present Position and Card Number 7—The Questioner. Card Number 6—Future Influence, and Card Number 3—Goal or Destiny, may reveal a trend in future possibilities. Card Number 9—Inner Emotions, frequently reveals an insight about the inner emotions, fears and anxieties of the questioner which helps explain the significance of the other revealed cards.

The relationship between several cards may indicate a trend or pattern. The cards may reveal the changing life pattern of the questioner and the areas of new direction into which he is advancing.

The descriptive names of the ten sequential spaces in the

card spread may vary slightly from reading to reading since the questioner may have one or more overlapping influences. Thus, the diviner should seek to interpret the cards, as spread, in the manner which feels most comfortable. Always bear in mind that the titles on the cards, the divinatory suggestions for each card, and the descriptive name of each of the ten sequential spaces in the card spread are meant as *suggestive* references. The diviner, through practice and intuition, should read the cards freely, allowing special interpretations and ideas to come to mind.

Frequently, the answer or guidance sought by the questioner at the time of the shuffling of the cards represents only a small portion of the total scope of the reading. The cards may suggest emotions, feelings and desires. They may stand for objects and persons. They may indicate circumstances and duration of time. The interpretation of each card, singularly and in connection with other cards, is limited only by the total responsiveness and capability of the diviner or interpreter. Thus, the cards frequently reveal a great deal about the questioner rather than solely responding to the original question.

After a reading is completed, and before starting a new reading, the diviner should remember to place the cards back in their original sequence in order to wipe away the currents and influences in the cards from the reading just completed. A questioner should be allowed no more than one reading per day so as to avoid any confusion which may arise due to continuously adjusting currents and influences. This is not meant to suggest that a second reading produces an interpretation inconsistent with the previous reading. Rather, influences and currents at one moment may vary in intensity with the next moment and cause confusion. One reading per day, per questioner, yields the most perceptive and concise reading.

The ten-card spread may also be employed with a forty-two-card pack by using the Major Arcana cards, the sixteen court cards and the four aces in each suit. Thus, the diviner should eliminate from the pack, the thirty-six cards numbered from 10 to 2 in each of the four suits.

Before the questioner shuffles the forty-two-card pack, the diviner should arrange the cards in the following sequence: The Ace of Swords, followed by the Page, Knight, Queen and King of that suit; the Ace of Wands, followed by the court cards in the same sequence; the Ace of Cups, and its court cards; the Ace of Pentacles, and its court cards. The Fool follows the King of Pentacles, and is followed by the numbered Major Arcana cards from I to XXI. Thus, the Ace of Swords lies face down on the table before shuffling.

CHAPTER VII

Spreading The Tarot Deck

THE TEN-CARD SPREAD described in the previous chapter is the most widely used for tarot card readings as well as one of the oldest known methods. It is the most effective spread utilizing only the Major Arcana cards, and it is occasionally employed with forty-two cards as previously described.

The Ten-Card Spread

The same ten-card spread may also be used while employing the entire seventy-eight-card tarot deck. The diviner first arranges the entire deck in the following sequence: The Sword suit Ace to King, Wand suit Ace to King, Cup suit Ace to King, and Pentacle suit Ace to King, followed by the Fool and the Major Arcana cards from I to XXI. Thus the Ace of Swords is the card which rests upon the table when the pack is placed face down before the questioner for shuffling.

MAJOR ARCANA

PENTACLES

CUPS

WANDS

SWORDS

Sequence of Full Tarot Deck

The procedures for the ten-card spread described in the previous chapter are then followed, using the full seventy-eight-card deck.

The Seven-Card Spread

The seven-card spread is especially useful to elicit a reply to a *yes* or *no* question. If four or more cards are inverted, the answer is usually no, or little likelihood of a yes, or a delayed yes.

The diviner puts the Major Arcana and Lesser Arcana cards in order, then separates them. The questioner then shuffles the Lesser Arcana cards and deals out the top eleven cards face down on top of the pile of Major Arcana cards. The forty-five remaining Lesser Arcana cards are set aside.

The questioner reshuffles the new pile of thirty-three cards (eleven Lesser Arcana and twenty-two Major Arcana) while repeating aloud the question to be answered.

The diviner then deals out the top seven cards face up from left to right as shown:

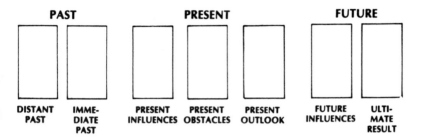

The Seven-Card Spread

PAST
DISTANT PAST: This card shows the broad and basic events and influences which have existed in the past life of the questioner and upon which many of the present events are taking place. It is the basis of fact which is embodied within the questioner and which results in a broad sense in his present outlooks, attitudes and areas of influence.

IMMEDIATE PAST: This card shows one or more recent events in the life of the questioner which have had a specific influence upon him and which have either just passed away or which are just passing away.

PRESENT
PRESENT INFLUENCES: This card is frequently connected to the previous card, Immediate Past. Present Influences show those influences or events which are acting upon the questioner at the present time and which are affecting his current outlook as represented in the subsequent two cards.

PRESENT OBSTACLES: This card represents the sphere of influence which constitutes an obstacle or hazard to the questioner. A seemingly favorable card may suggest a diversion or superfluous influence working upon the questioner and pulling him away from his true goals.

PRESENT OUTLOOK: This card is usually an extension of the previous cards, Present Influences tempered by Present Obstacles. This card indicates the possible extensions existing in the future based upon the current sphere of influence in which the questioner lives and works.

FUTURE

FUTURE INFLUENCES: This card is an extension of all the influences in the present circumstances of the questioner, plus the broad background of his past. It shows the sphere of influence that is coming into being in the near future in a general sense.

ULTIMATE RESULT: This card represents the culmination which will be brought about by all the previous influences as revealed by the cards in the divination provided events and influences continue as indicated without adjustment or alteration by the questioner within the limits possible.

The diviner reads the above seven cards based upon the sequential meanings described above. The symbolic pictures on the cards and the divinatory meanings for each card will result in a story indicating the past, present, and future of the questioner.

As previously stated, inverted cards are either weakened, delayed or reversed in meaning. If the first card is inverted then the diviner, instead of turning over each card from left to right, turns over the remaining top six cards from top to bottom.

The Name Spread

This spread utilizes that important aspect of an individual with which he has been associated and known since birth, his full name. The name spread utilizes the full tarot deck.

After the questioner shuffles the cards while simultaneously stating his question aloud, the diviner spreads the cards face up in the same number as the full name of the questioner.

For example, if the questioner's full name, comprising twenty-one letters, is ROBERT EDWIN SOUTHWORTH, the diviner spreads the first twenty-one cards in three rows from left to right as follows:

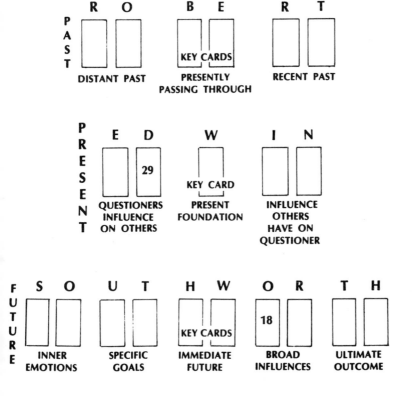

The Name Spread

If the questioner does not have a middle name, the number of cards in the first row are repeated in the middle row. If the questioner's first or middle name does not contain a minimum of three letters, or the last name a minimum of five letters, the rows are spread with three, three and five cards representing the first, middle and last names respectively. The center card in each row (or two cards if the row is even numbered) is the key card.

The top row represents the past influences and experiences which the questioner has experienced. To the left of the center key card are those influences from the distant past which represent the previous broad background of the questioner. To the right of the key card are those influences which the questioner has passed through during the relatively recent past, possibly during the past days, weeks or months. The key card represents those influences which are the most recent, either just past or just being completed.

The middle row of cards represents the period of present influences. To the left of the key card are those influences which the questioner exerts upon other people with whom he comes into contact. The cards also may show the impressions and opinions held by others about the questioner. To the right of the key card are those influences and pressures which other people exert upon the questioner. The center key card represents the foundation and environment in which the questioner is presently living and working.

The bottom row of cards relates to the future and ultimate outcome. To the left of the key card are the inner emotions and specific goals of the questioner. To the immediate right of the key card are the broad future influences or spheres of influence that are coming into being in the near future. To the extreme right are the ultimate outcome and final results which will be brought about from all of the influences as revealed by the other cards. The key card represents the immediate future in which the questioner is presently entering. This card may represent obstacles which will have to be met and overcome or it could represent opportunity, good fortune or progress towards a goal that the questioner is seeking to attain.

The name spread has one additional interesting feature, the *age card*. The age of the questioner is used to determine the *age card* which has strong meaning. For example, if the questioner, Robert Edwin Southworth, is eighteen years of age, then the diviner counts eighteen cards from left to right beginning at the top row, and the *age card* is found on the bottom row, seventh card from the left. If the questioner is 29 years of age, then the *age card* is the second card in the second row, see name spread illustration. The *age card* is usually a very strong and influential card. Its meaning is generally very important and a significant key to the past, present, or future of the questioner.

The Horseshoe Spread

The full deck of seventy-eight cards is shuffled face down by the questioner. The diviner then deals out the first card face down to his right on a part of the table designated pile A and two cards face down on a part of the table designated pile B. The diviner continues to deal out the deck face down at the rate of one card on pile A and two cards on pile B, until the entire deck is dealt out, leaving two piles consisting of twenty-six cards in pile A and fifty-two cards in pile B.

Pile A remains where it is for the moment. Pile B is picked up by the diviner and dealt face down into two new piles designated C and D at the rate of one card on pile C and two cards on pile D, one card on pile C and two cards on pile D, until the full fifty-two cards are dealt out thus leaving three piles: A = 26 cards, C = 18 cards and D = 34 cards.

The Diviner takes up pile D and deals face down two new piles designated E and F at the rate of one card on pile E and two cards on pile F, one card on pile E and two cards on pile F, until the full 34 cards are dealt out thus leaving four piles: A = 26 cards, C = 18 cards, E = 12 cards and F = 22 cards.

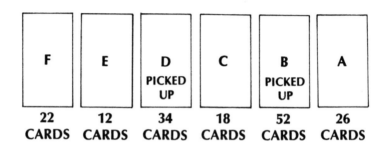

F	E	D PICKED UP	C	B PICKED UP	A
22 CARDS	12 CARDS	34 CARDS	18 CARDS	52 CARDS	26 CARDS

Six Card Piles for Horseshoe Spread

The diviner puts pile F aside, as these twenty-two cards are not to be used for reading. Pile A is picked up and the diviner deals out the twenty-six cards face up from *right* to *left* in the shape of a horseshoe, the first card being at the lowest right-hand corner of the horseshoe, and the twenty-sixth card being at the lowest left-hand corner, as illustrated.

The diviner reads the cards from *right* to *left* in a connected manner. When this is completed, the diviner reads the first and twenty-sixth cards together, the second and twenty-fifth cards together, etc., and so on until all the pairs have been read.

After completing the above reading, pile A is put aside and pile C is spread out and read exactly in the same way, and then pile E last.

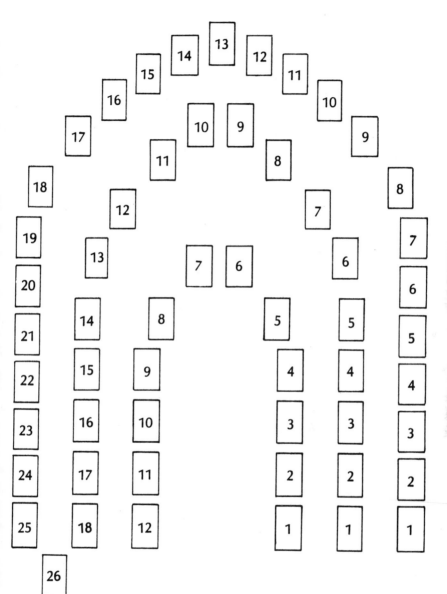

The Horseshoe Spread

The Royal Spread

This spread involves fifty-four cards: the Major Arcana cards, sixteen court cards (King, Queen, Knight and Page), four Aces, and pip cards numbered II, III and IIII in each suit.

To prepare this spread, the diviner first removes the twenty-four cards comprising Roman numerals V through X in each of the four suits.

The diviner then lets the questioner select from the court cards any one key card representing himself or herself and any one to four additional cards representing those persons either who have had in the past, or who presently have the greatest influence upon the questioner, or who are most involved in the question to which an answer is sought.

Generally, Swords represent dark-complexioned persons; Pentacles not so dark; Cups rather fair people; and Wands those much fairer. In making his selection, the questioner also considers those personal factors described under each of the cards in the previous section.

A man usually takes one of the Kings to represent himself; a woman, generally, one of the Queens. If the questioner is a youth or boy, he may select one of the Knights; while a young girl may select a Page. After the questioner selects the additional cards, he places face up the key card and the one to four additional court cards as shown.

The questioner then shuffles the remaining cards and the diviner places the cards face up (fifty-three to forty-nine cards, depending upon whether the questioner placed one to five cards on the table) beginning at the top row from *right* to *left*. The diviner proceeds to read the cards, combining groups of cards to form a series or sequence of events.

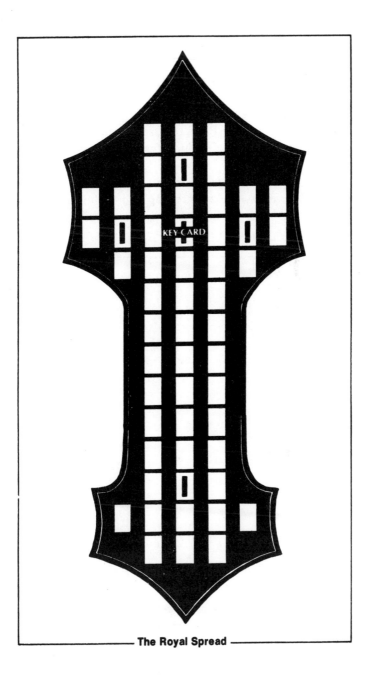

The Royal Spread

The Seventh-Card Spread

The questioner removes from the full deck one court card (King, Queen, Knight or Page) representing himself and places this key card on the table face upwards, leaving room to the left for seven more cards.

The questioner shuffles the cards face down and hands the pack to the diviner who places the top card face up to the left of the key card. The diviner then counts off six cards and transfers them, in the same order, to the bottom of the pack.

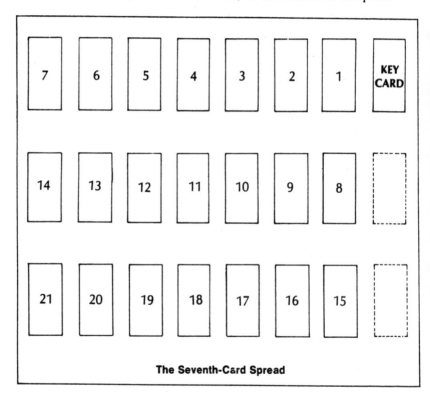

The Seventh-Card Spread

The seventh card is removed from the pack and placed to the left of the last spread card. This process is continued—six cards to the bottom of the pack and the seventh added to the spread—until the diviner has drawn a total of twenty-one cards by taking every seventh card and the twenty-one cards are arranged in three rows of seven cards each from *right* to *left*, always to the left of the key card.

The diviner reads the meaning of each card, and groups of cards, in sequence from *right* to *left*.

The Gypsy Spread

The diviner removes the Major Arcana cards from the tarot pack and gives to the questioner the fifty-six Lesser Arcana cards. The questioner shuffles the Lesser Arcana and separates, into a pile face down, the first twenty cards. These twenty Lesser Arcana cards are then put together with the Major Arcana cards to form a forty-two-card pack. The remaining thirty-six cards are set aside.

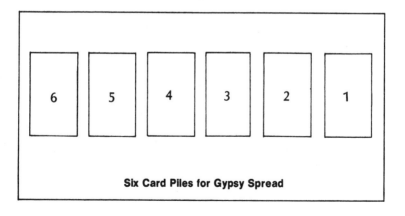

Six Card Piles for Gypsy Spread

The questioner shuffles the forty-two-card pack and separates the cards into six piles of seven cards each, placing them
face down, from *right* to *left,* so that the first seven cards form
the first pile, the second seven cards form the second pile, and
so on.

The diviner takes up each pile, beginning with the first, and
deals out the cards, face up, beginning from *right* to *left* in
rows of seven until there are six rows containing seven cards
each, as shown.

In this card spread, the questioner—if of the male sex—is
represented by any one of the following Major Arcana cards of
his choice: The Fool, The Magician, The Emperor. If the
questioner is of the female sex, she is represented by either the
High Priestess or The Empress.

The card representing the questioner is not taken from the
pack until the forty-two cards have been spread out as
previously directed. If the card sought is among the forty-two
cards spread on the table, it is removed and placed a slight
distance above and to the right of the first horizontal row. The
questioner then draws at random from the unused thirty-six-
card pack one card to fill the vacant position.

If the card sought is not among the forty-two exposed cards,
it is removed from the unused thirty-six-card pack and placed
above and to the right of the rows, as stated.

The cards are then read from *right* to *left* beginning at the
top row and continuing through each of the rows to card
number 7 on the bottom row. This reading will reveal a
general and continuous story of the questioner's past, present
and future. Generally, instead of reading each card individually, this spread is best interpreted if the diviner takes into
account adjoining cards or even an entire row of cards.
Sometimes it is worthwhile to run through the cards quickly,
so that the mind receives an overall general impression of the

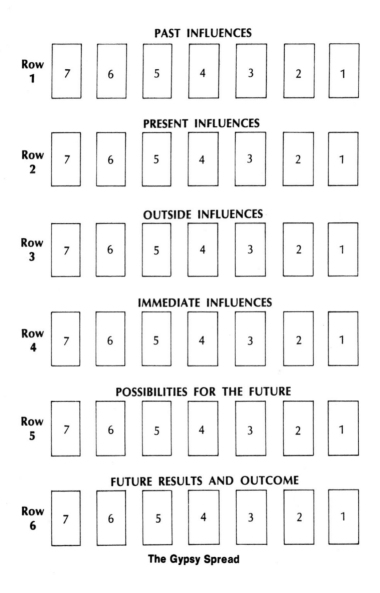

The Gypsy Spread

trend of the cards, and then the diviner reads the cards again in more detail. The cards should be adapted to harmonize with the conditions of the particular circumstances of the questioner such as age, sex, marital status, etc. The diviner should also bear in mind that the Major Arcana cards, and then the sixteen court cards, represent stronger and more compelling forces than the Lesser Arcana cards.

The meanings for each of the rows is as follows:

ROW 1—PAST INFLUENCES. Those influences and experiences which occurred in the past and which have played a part in life of the questioner.

ROW 2—PRESENT INFLUENCES. Those influences and experiences taking place at the present time in which the questioner is currently involved.

ROW 3—OUTSIDE INFLUENCES. Those influences, environmental factors, pressures and other outside events which are now taking place and over which the questioner has no control.

ROW 4—IMMEDIATE FUTURE INFLUENCES. Those events and influences which are approaching the questioner or into which he is presently entering, including unexpected events.

ROW 5—POSSIBILITIES FOR THE FUTURE. Those events and influences which are available, attainable and avoidable by the questioner if he wishes to prepare for them or avoid them.

ROW 6—FUTURE RESULTS AND OUTCOME. Those events and circumstances which will ultimately result in the future of the questioner.

✧◎ CHAPTER VIII ◎✧
Sample Tarot Card Readings

The following sample tarot card readings illustrate the ease with which the diviner may read and interpret the story of the cards using the ten-card spread, described earlier.

By way of brief review, the pack of seventy-eight cards is separated into two sections: the twenty-two Major Arcana cards and the fifty-six Lesser Arcana cards. The Lesser Arcana cards are then set aside. After placing the Major Arcana in sequence, the questioner shuffles them well while stating aloud his general question. At the conclusion of the shuffle, the questioner places the pack face down on the table.

The diviner turns over and places in the spread the top six cards and then the following four cards which he interprets bearing in mind the trend of the cards.

A reading, using the ten-card spread method, generally requires about twenty to thirty minutes. Depending upon the diviner's responsiveness, the interpretation of the cards singularly and in combination can be fairly extensive. Thus, each of the sample readings given in this chapter will vary to some extent, according to the perceptual and psychic talents of various diviners.

187

SAMPLE CARD SPREAD NO. 1

In this reading a middle-aged man is the questioner. He reveals to the diviner that recently he loaned a sum of money to a personal friend and business acquaintance who died suddenly. The man is now concerned whether the widow of the deceased will repay the loan, of which there is no written evidence. The widow of the deceased admits that her husband had mentioned borrowing an undisclosed amount of money from the questioner but she insists having no knowledge of whether or not her husband had repaid the money.

The sequence of the first six cards spread on the table by the diviner reveals the following:

The Present Position of the questioner is that a sudden and catastrophic event has taken place, in this case the death of his friend. In fact, the Death card appears in Card Position No. 1. Card Position No. 2, The Hanged Man, confirms that repayment of the loan has not been made and the lender has entered a period of uncertainty as to whether he will be repaid. Card Position No. 3, Judgment, forebodes someone taking advantage of the questioner, in this case either the deceased through unintentional circumstances or the deceased's widow by her possible decision not to repay the loan. Card Position No. 4, The Moon, and the following card, The Wheel of Fortune, confirm that the lender, however unwittingly, was deceived into making a loan for which repayment now appears uncertain. At the time of the loan the man may have thought he would reap a special gain. Card Position No. 6, The Magician, suggests, however, that the questioner through his ingenuity and capability may be able to influence the family of the deceased to repay the loan. Card Position No. 7, The Chariot, reveals the man's present concern and inner turmoil about the loan. Although the matter presently remains undecided, it could be favorably resolved through strong determination. Card Position No. 8, The Emperor, again reaffirms

CARD SPREAD NO. 1

Card No. 3
Goal
or
Destiny

Card No. 10
Final Result

Card No. 9
Inner Emotions

Card No. 6
Future
Influence

Card No. 1
Present
Position

Card No. 2

Immediate Influence

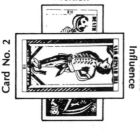

Card No. 4
Distant Past
Foundation

Card No. 8
Environmental
Factors

Card No. 5
Recent
Past Events

Card No. 7
The Questioner

the strong influence that the man will have over the family of
the deceased. Card Position No. 9, The Fool, reveals the
questioner's anxiety and apprehension about having made a
loan in a foolish manner. Card Position No. 10, Justice,
confirms that reasonableness and justice will prevail and that
the family of the deceased will repay the loan.

In summary, the cards clearly reveal the present circum-
stance of the death of the borrower, the uncertainty whether
the loan will be repaid, the strong influence of the lender
towards the family of the deceased and the ultimate favorable
outcome that he will be repaid. It is important that the
questioner act firmly when dealing with the deceased's family.
It is possible that a reading *before* the event might have
revealed the impending events, thus warning against making
the loan.

CARD SPREAD NO. 2

A rather young girl, the questioner, is recently divorced and
has custody of her two-year-old daughter. The questioner is
currently dating a young man who offers his hand in marriage.
The questioner feels she married foolishly the first time. She is
apprehensive and wonders if the outlook is more favorable for
her new romance.

Card Position No. 1, Temperance, confirms the questioner's
perception and concern about making any new accommo-
dations in life. She is, therefore, inclined to be more temperate
before making any rash decisions. Card Position No. 2,
Justice, further confirms the questioner's perception of a
possible unfavorable situation arising with her new boyfriend.
The Sun, Card Position No. 3, clearly indicates the young
girl's understandable need and desire for companionship and
marriage, suggesting the possibility she will rush into a new
romantic entanglement without sufficient consideration. Card

CARD SPREAD NO. 2

Card No. 3
Goal
or
Destiny

Card No. 10
Final Result

Card No. 9
Inner Emotions

Card No. 6
**Future
Influence**

Card No. 1
**Present
Position**

Card No. 2

Immediate
Influence

Card No. 4
**Distant Past
Foundation**

Card No. 8
**Environmental
Factors**

Card No. 5
**Recent
Past Events**

Card No. 7
The Questioner

Position Numbers 4 and 5, The Moon and The Hermit respectively, reveal the deception in the girl's previous marriage and her natural circumspection and apprehension towards any future marriage plans. Card Position No. 6, The Fool, confirms that the questioner tends to use poor judgment and sometimes evidences a lack of discipline. She is young, adventurous and lacks restraint. Card Position No. 7, The Hanged Man, reveals the current period of suspension and transition in the Questioner's life as evidenced by her being a divorcee with the additional problem of raising a child without the assistance of the father. The Wheel of Fortune, depicted in Card Position No. 8, confirms the presence of the new relationship and the possibility of eventual remarriage for good or bad. The girl's anxiety revealed in the Hierophant, Card Position No. 9, is one of timidity with the tendency to repeat previous mistakes. This is confirmed by the final card in Position No. 10, The Devil, which clearly indicates that marriage with the new acquaintance would prove disasterous for the questioner. She would find herself unhappy and in a subservient situation without love or understanding.

CARD SPREAD NO. 3

The questioner is a career girl from the far west presently living and working in a big eastern city. She dates frequently but there are no serious romantic interests in her life. She wonders whether she will succeed in her career and if her life includes an eventual marriage and a family.

Card Position No. 1, Temperance, suggests a highly regarded and worldly person with considerable confidence and intellectual capabilities. Card Position No. 2, The Hierophant, reveals that at times the questioner is inept in adapting to new circumstances and changing conditions especially personal

CARD SPREAD NO. 3

Card No. 10
Final Result

Card No. 9
Inner Emotions

Card No. 3
Goal
or
Destiny

Card No. 6
Future
Influence

Card No. 1
Present
Position

Card No. 2

Immediate
Influence

Card No. 4
Distant Past
Foundation

Card No. 8
Environmental
Factors

Card No. 5
Recent
Past Events

Card No. 7
The Questioner

relationships. Card Position No. 3, The Tower, suggests that a
sudden and unexpected event will take place, possibly a change
in careers or important advancement. The Emperor in Card
Position No. 4, followed by Card Position No. 5, Justice,
suggests that the questioner was dominated as a child,
probably by her father or some other male influence. The
Empress, Card Position No. 6, suggests that another person,
possibly a female for whom the young woman works, will
wield a strong influence over the questioner's future career.
The strong capability and creativity of the career girl is
confirmed by Card Position No. 7, The Magician. Card
Position No. 8, The Devil, especially when viewed in conjunction with The Empress, suggests that the person who will
wield future influence over the young woman does not have her
best interests at heart. The questioner has an inkling of this
problem as revealed by her inner emotions and anxieties, The
Moon, in Card Position No. 9. The final result, Card Position
No. 10, The Wheel of Fortune, indicates neither a firm yes or
no answer to the young woman's question but rather the
foreboding that another person holds the fate of the questioner's future career. The career girl, therefore, is urged to exert
stronger efforts in her own behalf. There is nothing indicated
in the cards with respect to the possibility of marriage, since
the questioner appears entirely involved at present with her
career, at the expense of her romantic life.

CARD SPREAD NO. 4

The questioner is a mature executive employed by a large
company. He is planning to leave his employment and enter
into his own business venture involving considerable capital
investment. The questioner has never been in business for
himself and is somewhat apprehensive about embarking on his
own. His wife feels that her husband should do whatever will
make him happiest.

CARD SPREAD NO. 4

Card No. 3
Goal
or
Destiny

Card No. 10
Final Result

Card No. 9
Inner Emotions

Card No. 6
Future
Influence

Card No. 1
Present
Position

Card No. 2

Immediate
Influence

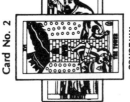

Card No. 4
Distant Past
Foundation

Card No. 8
Environmental
Factors

Card No. 5
Recent
Past Events

Card No. 7
The Questioner

Card Position No. 1, The Hermit, suggests that the questioner is somewhat introspective and perhaps not the type of person who enjoys working as a team member in a large company. This card may also indicate that the steps he has taken with respect to leaving his employment may prove temporarily regressive or difficult at the onset. Card Position No. 2, The Tower, confirms the questioner's plans to break from his present employment arrangements and to go into business for himself. Card Position No. 3, The Star, is very favorable and indicates rising opportunity and favorable prospects. The past circumstances surrounding the questioner revealed in Card Position No. 4, The Wheel of Fortune, have been fortuitous in opportunity. Card Position No. 5, The Fool, confirms the questioner's desire to embark on a new adventure while suggesting the necessity of careful planning and cautious action so as not to fall from the precipice of success. The future influence of the questioner, shown in Card Position No. 6, The Empress, indicates that another person, presumably his wife, will offer strong favorable assistance in the new undertaking, while Card Position No. 7, Temperance, reveals that the questioner will both recognize and utilize the assistance and opportunities available to him towards attaining his goal. Card Position No. 8, The Hierophant, confirms the capability and wisdom of the questioner but also indicates a tendency to cling to the past. Perhaps this explains why he has not gone into business for himself earlier. Card Position No. 9, The Moon, reveals the man's personal anxiety and inner concern about investing in his own business. Card Position No. 10, The Sun, confirms the overall impression that the questioner, in conjunction with strong and favorable feminine assistance, will succeed in his new venture and it is, therefore, recommended that he go into business for himself.

CARD SPREAD NO. 5

The questioner is a dynamic young man recently graduated from college and starting employment with a large law firm. Well-dressed and well-spoken, he evidences considerable enthusiasm about the future. He wishes to know what the future holds as revealed by the tarot cards.

Card Position No. 1, The Magician, indicates the young man's skill and capability as well as imaginative self-reliance. He is embarking upon the great adventure of his life. Card Position No. 2, The Chariot, suggests that a possible voyage or journey will take place in the near future. However, the young man is impetuous. He should pay attention to details while maintaining a proper balance in his work to avoid being torn in too many different directions. Card Position No. 3, The Empress, indicates that a possible engagement or marriage may be in the offing in the near future. The voyage previously indicated seemingly would be a honeymoon. Card Position Numbers 4 and 5, Strength and The Sun respectively, confirm the strong and favorable upbringing of the young man in a generally happy and satisfactory childhood. Card Position No. 6, Judgment, indicates that there will be considerable self-development and promotion for the young man if he maintains himself in proper honesty and conduct. Card Position No. 7, The Emperor, confirms the strong capabilities of the young man who is intelligent and possesses the quality of leadership. Card Position No. 8, The Lovers, confirms with Card Position No. 3, The Empress, the strong possibility of an impending engagement or marriage. Card Position No. 9, The World, reveals the young man's strong motivation for achieving success and power. Card Position No. 10, The Fool, reveals the overall conclusion that the young man is very capable and ambitious. The young man's cards indicate a strong favorable reading but he should be careful not to make any foolish moves in the future which might divert him from his ultimate destiny or possibly even cause him unnecessary failure.

CARD SPREAD NO. 6

A sixteen-year-old boy is the questioner. He does not ask any specific question but rather would like to know the general future outlook. He states that he does not know what he wants to do in life. He feels that nothing sufficiently challenges him. He wonders in what field of activity he should devote his future efforts.

Card Position No. 1, The Chariot, confirms the present divided position of the questioner. Similar to the two horses pulling apart, he is in conflict and turmoil. The young man needs strong supervision. Card Position No. 2, Temperance, suggests that his present supervision is one of over-moderation and frugality. Possibly his home life is without stimulation. Card Position No. 3, The Empress, indicates that a strong person will dominate the young man in later life, possibly a strong and nagging wife or an over-protective mother. Card Position No. 4, Death, reveals that some sudden and abrupt change occured in the boy's past life, such as the death of his father, or someone for whom he had great admiration, or possibly financial failure of the family. Card Position No. 5, The Lovers, indicates the tendency of the boy to maintain a mother image and to remain tied to his mother's dominance. Card Position No. 6, The Sun, indicates the young man's sincere desire to live a complacent and satisfactory life without conflict or adversity. The Hanged Man, Card Position No. 7, confirms his complete indecision with respect to his future endeavors. He is in a state of suspension and transition. Card Position No. 8, The High Priestess, indicates that a strong

CARD SPREAD NO. 5

Card No. 10
Final Result

Card No. 3
Goal
or
Destiny

Card No. 9
Inner Emotions

Card No. 6
Future
Influence

Card No. 1
Present
Position

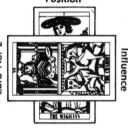
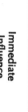

Card No. 2

Immediate
Influence

Card No. 4
Distant Past
Foundation

Card No. 8
Environmental
Factors

Card No. 5
Recent
Past Events

Card No. 7
The Questioner

person, again probably his mother, maintains a dominating influence over him. Card Position No. 9, The Magician, reveals that the young man experiences moments of apprehension as to his own capabilities to succeed in life. This may explain in part his dependence upon his mother and his indecision as to the future. Card Position No. 10, Strength, is the key to the future for the youth. It underscores his urgent need to develop stronger individual traits if he is to lead a happy and successful life as an individual.

CARD SPREAD NO. 7

A young married woman with no children wishes to know the outlook for her future. She recently took new employment as a secretary for an advertising agency and she enjoys her job. Her marriage is happy but she feels that her life is without meaningful direction.

Card Position No. 1, The Empress, indicates that the young woman is a very capable and efficient worker. Card Position No. 2, The High Priestess, indicates that she is also intellectual, possesses the ability to teach and instruct others and is independent-minded. Card Position No. 3, The Hierophant, indicates that although the young woman is self-reliant she tends to lean towards other individuals for guidance and understanding, possibly a religious person or someone with whom she works. Card Position No. 4, Temperance, indicates that through self-control and the ability to fully utilize her capabilities, the young woman leads an organized life. Recently, as evidenced by Card Position No. 5, The Magician, she has become more creative and self-expressive with the desire to break away from some of the bonds which she feels restrain her. This is confirmed by Card Position No. 6, The Fool, which indicates this trend will continue and she will tend to be more adventurous and possibly frivolous. Card Position

CARD SPREAD NO. 6

Card No. 10
Final Result

Card No. 3
Goal
or
Destiny

Card No. 9
Inner Emotions

Card No. 6
Future
Influence

Card No. 1
Present
Position

Card No. 2

Immediate
Influence

Card No. 4
Distant Past
Foundation

Card No. 8
Environmental
Factors

Card No. 5
Recent
Past Events

Card No. 7
The Questioner

No. 7, Justice, indicates that the woman possesses integrity and is always fair and honest. Card Position No. 8, The Chariot, indicates that someone, possibly her husband, a member of her family or a friend, is pulling her in a different direction from her previous interests. The change will be for better or for worse depending upon the young woman's intentions. Card Position No. 9, The Wheel of Fortune, indicates that the young woman feels that unexpected events will soon occur. From the trend of the cards in the card spread, these events will probably be favorable and connected to the symbolic picture on the last card, The Emperor, which indicates that the young woman's fortune is closely tied to another person, probably her husband, to whom her life is devoted and her love is constant.

CARD SPREAD NO. 7

Card No. 10
Final Result

Card No. 3
Goal
or
Destiny

Card No. 9
Inner Emotions

Card No. 6
Future
Influence

Card No. 1
Present
Position

Card No. 4
Distant Past
Foundation

Card No. 2

Immediate
Influence

Card No. 8
Environmental
Factors

Card No. 5
Recent
Past Events

Card No. 7
The Questioner

A Selective Annotated Bibliography

This comprehensive listing comprises one hundred and nine books selected from among the most important works dealing with tarot cards in all their aspects from the year 1540 to the present. Books designated with an asterisk (*) are from the private collection of the author.

*Alta, Elie. *Le Tarot Egyptien. Ses Symboles, Ses Nombres, Son Alphabet. Comment on lit Le Tarot.* (Includes reproduction of works by M. M. d'Odoucet). Vichy, France. 1922. 8vo. Illustrated. Text in French. 311 pages.

> Alta supports the Egyptian origin of tarot cards. Text includes information about Etteilla, origin and meaning of each of the Major Arcana and Minor Arcana cards, and lessons in the application of tarot as presented in 1793 by d'Odoucet, student and collabora-

tor of Etteilla, whose published work, *Science Des Signes, Où Medecine de l'Esprit, connue sous le nom d'Art de tirer les Cartes,* is reproduced in the Alta book beginning at page 238.

*Bargagli, Girolamo. *Dialogo de Givochi che nelle Vegghie Sanesi si vsano di fare.* Siena. 1572. 8vo. Text in Italian. 223 pages.

Contains, on page 77, the earliest printed reference to the game of Tarocchi. "And I also have seen the game of Tarocchi played, with all present being given a Tarocchi name, and someone after declaring, asking that, for any reason whatsoever, the name of a particular tarocco card be given to this one or that one." A rare collector's item.

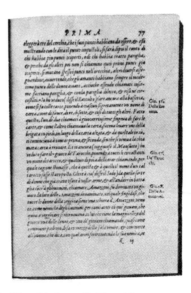

Title Page and Page 77 from *Dialogo de Givochi che nelle Vegghie Sanesi si vsano di fare.* Girolamo Bargagli. 1572.

*Benham, W. Gurney. *Playing Cards. History of The Pack and Explanations of its Many Secrets.* London. 1931. 8vo. Illustrated. 196 pages.

> Includes a section on early tarot cards and the symbolic meanings of the pack.

*Bennett, Sidney. *Tarot For The Millions.* California. 1967. 8vo. 157 pages.

> Presents various card spreads and sample tarot readings along with description and meanings for each of the Major and Lesser Arcana cards.

*Boiteau, P. d'Ambly. *Les Cartes à Jouer et La Cartomancie.* Paris. 1854. 16mo. Illustrated. Text in French. 390 pages.

> Describes the origin of cards, history of tarot cards, and includes a complete section on cartomancy including anecdotes about Mlle. Le Normand, the famous French sibyl, and an appendix containing Etteilla's method for fortune-telling with cards.

*British Museum. *Playing Cards of Various Ages and Countries.* Selected from The Collection of Lady Charlotte Schreiber. London. 1892-1895. 3 Volumes. Folio.

> Profusely illustrated. This comprehensive collection on playing cards includes reproductions in black and white of many tarot cards from decks produced throughout Europe during the 16th to 19th centuries. Very rare collector's item.

*Brown, Wenzell, *How To Tell Fortunes With Cards.* New York. 1969. 12mo. Illustrated. 128 pages.

> Describes the meaning of each of the pip cards. Includes several sample spreads.

*Bullet, Jean Baptiste. *Recherches Historiques Sur Les Cartes à Jouer avec des Notes Critiques & Intéressantes.* Lyon. 1757. 12mo. Text in French. 163 pages.

Describes the origin of playing cards with specific

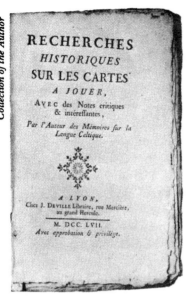

Collection of the Author

Title Page from
*Recherches Historiques
Sur Les Cartes à Jouer.*
Jean Baptiste Bullet. 1757.

reference to published works during the Middle Ages
which possibly may relate to cards and their introduction into Europe. Rare collector's item.

*Case, Paul Foster. *The Book of Tokens: Tarot Meditations.*
California. 1934. 12mo. Illustrated. 200 pages.
Comprises meditations on the occult meaning of the
twenty-two Hebrew letters, illustrated by the twenty-
two Major Tarot Keys.

* ——— .*The Tarot. A Key to the Wisdom of the Ages.*
Virginia. 1947. Reprint. 12mo. Illustrated. 214 pages.
Describes each of the Major Arcana cards, occult
meaning of numbers, methods of study and tarot
divination.

* ——— . *A Brief Analysis of The Tarot.* New York. 1927.
8vo. Without illustrations. 102 pages.
Same text as: *The Tarot. A Key to the Wisdom of the
Ages.*

*Chatto, William Andrew. *Facts and Speculations on the Origin and History of Playing Cards.* London. 1848. 8vo. Illustrated. 343 pages.

> Describes the origin of playing cards including the premise that the twenty-two Major Arcana cards and the remaining suit cards were once separate· and afterwards combined. Includes references to the introduction of cards into Europe and the various conflicting theories as to their origin. Collector's item.

*Cicognara, Leopoldo. *Memorie Spettanti Alla Storia Della Calcografia del Commend.* Prato. 1831. 8vo. Text in Italian. 262 pages.

> Describes the origin of playing cards including detailed commentary on early tarocchi decks. A separate volume totaling eighteen pages in folio includes numerous reproductions in black and white of early Italian card designs.

Court de Gebelin, Antoine. *Le Monde Primitif, analysé et comparé avec le monde moderne.* Volume I, commencing at Page 363: *Du Jeu des Tarots. Où l'on traite de son origine, où on explique ses allégories, et où l'on fait voir qu'il est la source de nos cartes modernes à jouer,* etc., etc. Paris 1775 to 1784. Nine volumes. Text in French.

> This famous dissertation on tarot cards describes the Egyptian origin of the cards, the manner in which Gebelin first became introduced to the cards, the meaning of each of the Major Arcana cards and the manner in which the cards subsequently spread to Europe. Rare collector's item.

*Crowley, Aleister. *The Book of Thoth* (Egyptian Tarot). New York. 1969. Reprint. 8vo. Illustrated. 287 pages.

> Describes the theory of tarot including its Egyptian origin and relationship to the Holy Kabbalah, meaning of each of the Major and Lesser Arcana cards, plus

Crowley's pictorial interpretation of each of the cards.

*D'Allemagne, Henry-René. *Les Cartes à Jouer du Quatorzième au Vingtième Siècle. Contenant 3200 reproductions de cartes, dont 956 en couleur, 12 planches hors textes coloriées a l'aquarelle, 25 phototypies, 116 enveloppes illustrées pour jeux de cartes et 340 vignettes et vues diverses.* Paris. 1906. Folio. 2 Volumes. Text in French. Tome I—504 pages. Tome II—640 pages.

Cover from *Les Cartes à Jouer du Quatorzième au Vingtième Siècle.* Henry-René D'Allemagne. 1906.

One of the most authoritative books on the history of playing cards. Includes various references to the origin of tarot cards, reproductions in black and white and full color of different tarot cards, and a chapter on the use of cards for divination from early times until the 20th century. Rare collector's item.

*Deutsches Spielkarten Museum. *Tarocke Mit Franzosischen Farben*. Germany. 1969. 8vo. Illustrated. Text in German. 60 pages.

> Contains a description of 375 different packs of cards, mostly tarot decks with some other types, which were displayed at an exhibit between July 2, 1967 and April 15, 1968 at The Deutsches Spielkarten Museum in Bielefeld, West Germany.

*Doane, Doris Chase and King Keyes. *Tarot-Card Spread Reader*. New York. 1970. Reprint. 8vo. Illustrated. 207 pages.

> Describes tarot cards and how to use them. Provides examples of tarot card readings and the key phrases for the seventy-eight cards in the tarot pack. Includes section on astrological symbolism. Also reprinted under the title *How To Read Tarot Cards*.

*Duchartre, Pierre Louis. *Tarots Packs. Tarockspiele. Jeux de Tarots*. Graphis Magazine. Zurich. 1949. Volume 5. No. 26. Text in French.

> Six-page illustrated article starting at page 168 in *Graphis Magazine* describing the graphic development of French tarot cards.

*Duchesne, Jean l'aine. *Jeux de Cartes Tarots et de Cartes Numérales, du quatorzième au dix-huitième siècle. Publiés par la Société des Bibliophiles Francais*. Paris. 1844. Folio. Hand illustrated. Text in French. 100 pages. *Petit papier*.

> Only thirty-two copies on *grande papier* and one hundred copies on *petit papier* were published. Contains hand-illuminated reproductions of the seventeen tarot cards in the Bibliotheque Nationale in Paris which are believed by some scholars to have been painted by Jacquemin Gringonneur for Charles VI of France in 1392. Also includes reproductions of fifty

tarots from Italy, the so-called Tarocchi de Mantegna from copper plates. Very rare collector's item.

Collection of the Author

Title Page from
*Jeux de Cartes
Tarots et de
Cartes Numérales.*
Jean l'aine Duchesne.
1844.

*Edindustria Editoriale. *Antiche Carte Italiane da Tarocchi.* Rome. 1961. Folio. Illustrated. Text in Italian. 26 pages. Contains a brief history of ancient Italian tarot cards with full color reproductions from early Tarot, Tarocchino and Minchiate packs. Second edition limited to three hundred copies.

*Etteilla (Alliette). *Les Sept Nuances de L'Oeuvre Philosophique—Hermetique, Suivies d'un Traite sur La Perfection des Metaux, mis sous l'Avant-Titre L.D.D.P.* 1772. 48 pages. L.D.D.P. ou La Perfection des Metaux. 60 pages.

Frontispiece and Title Page from *Manière de se Récréer avec le Jeu de Cartes Nommées Tarots.* Etteilla. 1783.

This book and the following volumes comprise the works of Etteilla, disciple of Court de Gebelin. Includes Egyptian origin of tarot cards and the secret methods of spreading and interpreting them popularized by Etteilla. Texts in French. Very rare collector's items.

* ———— . *Philosophie des Hautes Sciences, ou La Clef Donnée aux Enfans de l'Art de la Science & de la Sagesse.* Amsterdam. 1785. 189 pages.

* ———— . *Manière de se Récréer avec le Jeu de Cartes Nommées Tarots. Pour servir de premier Cahier à cet Ouvrage.* Amsterdam. 1783. 182 pages.

* ———— . *Manière de se Récréer avec le Jeu de Cartes Nommées Tarots. Pour servir de second Cahier à cet Ouvrage.* Amsterdam. 1785. 202 pages.

* ———— . *Manière de se Récréer avec le Jeu de Cartes*

Nommées Tarots. Pour servir de troisième Cahier à cet Ouvrage. Amsterdam. 1783. 142 pages.

* ———— . *Fragment sur Les Hautes Sciences, Suivi D'une Note sur les trois fortes de Médecines données aux Hommes, dont une mal-a-propos délaissée.* Amsterdam. 1785. 60 pages.

* ———— . *Jeu des Tarots ou Le Livre de Thot, ouvert à la Manière des Egyptiens, pour servir ici, a L'Inter-prétation de tous les Rêves, Songes et Visions diurnes et nocturnes.* 12 pages.

* ———— . *Livre de Thot.* 1789. 4 pages.

* ———— . *Manière de se Récréer avec le Jeu de Cartes Nommées Tarots. Pour servir de quatrième Cahier à cet Ouvrage.* Amsterdam. 1785. 256 pages.

* ———— . *Sciences Leçons Théoriques et Pratiques du Livre de Thot. Moyennes Classes.* Amsterdam. 1787. 94 pages.

* ———— . *Science Leçons Théoriques et Pratiques du Livre de Thot.* 1787. 24 pages.

*Falconnier, R. *Les XXII Lames Hermétiques du Tarot Divinatoire. Exactement reconstituées d'apres les textes sacrés et selon la tradition des Mages de l'ancienne Egypte.* Paris. 1896. 12mo. Illustrated. Text in French. 104 pages.

Describes the Egyptian origin of tarot cards and the meaning of each card for purposes of divination. Illustrations of cards are pictures with Egyptian influence.

*Franck, Adolphe. *The Kabbalah. The Religious Philosophy of the Hebrews.* New York. 1967. Reprint. 12mo. 224 pages.

Describes the ancient origins of the Kabbalah and its two principal works, *Sefer Yetzirah* and the *Zohar.*

*Gardner, Richard. *Evolution Through The Tarot.* England. 1970. 8vo. Reprint. 112 pages.

Reprint of the book previously published under the title *Accelerate Your Evolution.* Describes the twenty-two

Major Arcana cards in metaphysical terms.

*Ginsburg, Christian D. *The Essenes. Their History and Doctrines. The Kabbalah. Its Doctrines, Development and Literature.* London. 1970. Reprint. 12mo. 245 pages.

> *The Kabbalah* was first published in 1863 and *The Essenes* in 1864. Describes the meaning of the Kabbalah including its origin, development and application as The Tree of Life.

*Girault, Francis. *Mlle. Le Normand. Sa Biographie, Ses Prédictions Extraordinaires, son commerce avec les personnages les plus illustres d'Europe, de la République, du Directoire, de l'Empire et de la Restauration jusju'a nos jours; La Chiromancie et La Cartomancie expliquées par la Pythenisse du XIX siecle. Avec une Introduction philosophique sur les Sciences occultes mises en regard des sciences naturelles.* Paris. 1843. 16mo. Illustrated. Text in French. 191 pages.

> Relates the life of the famous French sibyl Mlle. Le Normand, whose fame was renowned during the Napoleon era. Includes a description of the seventy-eight cards of the tarot pack.

Gray, Eden. *Mastering The Tarot. Basic lessons in an ancient, mystic art.* New York. 1971. Illustrated. 8vo. 160 pages.

> This beginner's book teaches the meanings of the individual cards and the various methods of reading them. Includes significance of each card within the card spread, relationships to numerology and actual sample readings.

* —— . *A Complete Guide to the Tarot.* New York. 1970. Reprint. 4to. Illustrated. 156 pages.

> Describes the Major and Minor Arcana cards, methods of reading the cards and occult philosophy as it relates

to tarot including numerology, astrology and the Kabbalah.

* ⸺ . *The Tarot Revealed: A Modern Guide to Reading the Tarot Cards*. New York. 1969. Reprint. 12mo. Illustrated. 239 pages.

Includes chapters on the magic of the cards, descriptions of the Minor and Major Arcana, divination with the tarot cards, meditations, specimen readings and glossary of symbols.

*Grimaud, B. P. *Grand Etteilla Egyptian Gypsies Tarot*. Paris. 1969. 48mo. 118 pages.

Instruction booklet which accompanies Grand Etteilla cards produced by France-Cartes/J.M. Simon of Paris. Describes each of the seventy-eight cards in the Etteilla deck including significance of the cards next to each other.

* ⸺ . *Tarot of Marseilles*. 1969. 48mo. Paris. 48 pages.

Instruction booklet which accompanies the Tarot of Marseilles deck produced by France-Cartes/J.M. Simon of Paris. Describes how to use tarot cards, and includes the meanings of the Major and Lesser Arcana cards.

*Hargrave, Catherine Perry. *A History of Playing Cards and a Bibliography of Cards and Gaming*. New York. 1930. 4to. Profusely illustrated. 468 pages.

Describes origin of playing cards with sections on tarot cards as developed in different European countries. Many illustrations. Excellent bibliography from the library of United States Playing Card Company.

*Hasbrouck, Muriel Bruce. *Pursuit of Destiny*. New York. 1941. 8vo. Illustrated. 270 pages.

Describes the tarot pack as it relates to a specific period of time within the solar year. The author attempts to assign one tarot card for each ten-day cycle period.

*Heline, Corinne. *The Bible and the Tarot.* California. 1969. 8vo. Illustrated. 237 pages.

> Contains the basic principles of the tarot pack including letters, numbers, ciphers and codes, description of the Kabbalah and the Tetragrammaton. Emphasis is placed upon the Hebrew alphabet. Pictures are ancient Egyptian designs.

*Hoy, David. *The Meaning of Tarot.* Tennessee. 1971. 8vo. Illustrated. 168 pages.

> Describes the tarot deck including preparations for divination, methods of divination and meanings of each of the cards.

*Huber und Herpel. *Bologneser Tarockspiel des 17. Jahrhunderts. Gioseppe Maria Mitelli.* Germany. 1970. Text in French with some English, Italian and German. Folio. Illustrated. 8 pages.

> One hundred and fifty copies printed. Reproduces the Tarocchino of Bologna cards designed by Gioseppe Maria Mitelli in the 17th century.

*Huson, Paul. *The Devil's Picturebook. The Compleat Guide to Tarot Cards.* New York. 1971. 8vo. Illustrated. 256 pages.

> Describes the Major Arcana and the Minor Arcana cards and presents the methods of laying out the cards and reading the pack. Includes a description of the origin of tarot cards.

*Kaplan, S. R. (Stuart R.). *Tarot Cards For Fun And Fortune Telling.* New York. 1970. 8vo. Illustrated. 96 pages.

> Illustrated guide to the spreading and interpretation of the popular seventy-eight-card tarot IJJ deck of Muller & Cie, Switzerland. Contains an introduction to tarot, meaning of each of the Major and Lesser Arcana cards and eight methods of spreading the cards including an ancient ten-card spread which gives a clear and concise reading.

Collection of the Author

Cover From *Tarot
Cards for Fun
and Fortune Telling.*
S. R. Kaplan. 1970.

Collection of the Author

Cover from
*Official Rules
of the Tarotrump
Card Game.*
Stuart R. Kaplan. 1971.

*Kaplan, Stuart R. *Official Rules of the Tarotrump Card Game.* U.S. Games Systems, Inc. New York. 1971.

The complete rules of the game of Tarotrump based upon the original rules of the popular 16th-century Italian games of Minchiate and Tarocchi slightly modified for today's playing card enthusiast. Includes sample hands by Jeff Rubens.

* ———— . *Tarot Classic.* New York. 1972. 8vo. Illustrated.
256 pages.

The classic guide to the tarot pack. Describes the
current phenomenal interest in tarot, the ancient origin
of the cards and the earliest known European references to tarot, the oldest packs still in existence, the
development of tarot by Gebelin, Etteilla, Levi, Papus
and Waite, the complete divinatory meaning of each of
the Major Arcana and Lesser Arcana cards, and
sample card spreads and methods of divination. Illustrated with the Major Arcana and court cards from the
famous Tarot Classic deck. Contains an extensive
bibliography of noteworthy and rare books on tarot
from the author's private collection.

*Kasdin, Simon. *The Esoteric Tarot.* New Jersey. 1965. 8vo.
Illustrated. 96 pages.

Describes the twenty-two Major Arcana cards using
unusual symbols with specific reference to the Hebrew
alphabet and the Sepher Yetzerah.

*Knight, Gareth. *A Practical Guide to Qabalistic Symbolism.*
Volume I—*On the Spheres of the Tree of Life.* 249 pages.
Volume II—*On the Paths and the Tarot.* 291 pages.
England. 1965.

Describes the application and theory of Kabbalistic
symbolism and analyzes the Major Arcana cards from
the standpoint of tarot symbols, Hebrew letters and
astrological signs.

*Laurence, L. W. de. *The Illustrated Key to the Tarot.* 1971.
This book is a reprint version of the famous Waite
book: *The Key to the Tarot* (see Waite).

*Le Normand, Mlle. M.A. *Les Souvenirs Prophétiques
D'Une Sibylle, Sur les Causes Sécrètes de son Ar-
restation, Le 11 Décembre 1809.* Paris. 1814. Text in
French. 590 pages.

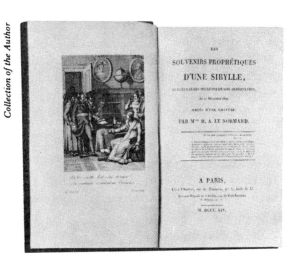

Collection of the Author

Frontispiece and Title Page from *Les Souvenirs Prophetiques D'une Sibylle*. Mlle. M. A. LeNormand. 1814.

Describes the causes and events leading to Mlle. Le Normand's arrest and imprisonment ordered by Napoleon. Includes Mlle. Le Normand's revelation to Empress Josephine of her eventual divorce by Napoleon because of the Emperor's desire for a male heir.

*Levi, Eliphas (Alphonse Louis Constant). *Dogme et Rituel de la Haute Magie*. Paris. 1854.

The works of Eliphas Levi were published in the second half of the nineteenth century and deal with the Kabbalah, occultism, mysticism and the tarot as a sacred book. Texts in French. However, English reprints are available.

* ———— . *Histoire de la Magie*. Paris. 1860.
* ———— . *La Clef des Grands Mystères*. Paris. 1861.
* ———— . *Le Livre des Splendeurs*. Paris. 1894.
* ———— . *Clefs Magiques et Clavicules de Salomon*. 1895.
* ———— . *Le Grand Arcane ou L'Occultisme Dévoilé*. Paris. 1898.

*Lhôte, Jean-Marie. *Le Tarot. Discours en forme de catalogue a propos d'une exposition sur les Tarots realisée par la Maison de la Culture d'Amiens.* Paris. 1971. 4to. Illustrated. Text in French. 55 pages.

> Describes an exhibit on the history and development of tarot cards presented by the Maison de la Culture, Amiens, France in the spring of 1971.

*Lind, Frank. *How To Understand The Tarot.* London. 1969. Illustrated. 63 pages.

> Describes the Major Arcana cards with some references to the Lesser Arcana cards and methods of divination.

*Mann, Sylvia. *Collecting Playing Cards.* New York. 1966. 8vo. Illustrated. 215 pages.

> A helpful reference book on playing cards including references to early tarot cards produced in European countries and suggestions for identifying standard packs.

Marcolini, Francesco. *Le Sorti di Francesco Marcolini da Forli, intitulate Giardino di Pensieri, allo Illustrissimo Signore Hercole Estense, Duca di Ferrar.* Venice. 1540. Illustrated. Text in Italian.

> One of the earliest known books employing cards for divination. Contains 99 woodcuts. Depicts the suit of deniers. Questions are answered depending upon a kind of oracular triplet to which one is directed based upon the drawing of one or two cards. A second edition was published in 1550.

*Marteau, Paul. *Le Tarot de Marseille.* Paris. 1949. 4to. Illustrated. Text in French. 281 pages.

> Describes the significance of each of the twenty-two Major Arcana cards. Each section includes a full-color card facsimile from the Tarot of Marseille pack pasted to the page. Includes methods of divination.

* Mathers, S. L. MacGregor. *The Tarot, Its Occult Significa-
tion, Use in Fortune-telling, and Method of Play.*
London. 1888. 24 mo. 60 pages.

Describes the origin of the tarot deck, meaning of each
card, rules (incomplete) for the game of tarot, and
several methods of card spreading used for divination.

* Mayananda. *The Tarot For Today.* Being Notes Relative to
the Twenty-two Paths of the Tree of Life and the Tarot
Trumps Together with a new way of approach to this
Ancient Symbol, more suited to the present Aquarian Age
and entitled The Horus Arrangement. London. 1963.
8vo. Illustrated. 255 pages.

Describes the origin of tarot cards, description of each
of the Major Arcana, symbolism, tradition and Kabbalistic applications.

* Merlin, R. *Origine des Cartes à Jouer. Recherches Nouvelles
Sur Les Naïbes, Les Tarots et Sur Les Autres Espèces de
Cartes.* Paris. 1869. 4to. Illustrated. Text in French. 144
pages plus 74-page Album.

Describes the various possible origins of playing cards
including details on the inaccuracies of prior research.
Contains a large album of reproductions of many cards
including Tarocchi of Mantegna cards, Minchiate of
Florence cards and various ancient tarot decks from
France and Italy. Collector's item.

* Moakley, Gertrude. *The Tarot Cards Painted by Bonifacio
Bembo for the Visconti-Sforza Family.* An Iconographic
and Historical Study. New York. 1966. 8vo. Illustrated.
124 pages.

Describes the Visconti-Sforza tarocchi cards (circa
1450) originally owned by the Fourth Duke of Milan,
Francesco Sforza. Seventy-four of seventy-eight cards
still exist today and they are described in considerable
detail.

*Moakley, Gertrude. *The Waite-Smith "Tarot."* Bulletin of The New York Public Library. New York. October 1954. Volume 58. Number 10. 12mo. Illustrated. Pages 471-475.

> Describes the reference to tarot cards by T. S. Eliot in his poem *The Waste Land* and the contemporary tarot deck drawn by Pamela Colman Smith under the direction of Arthur E. Waite.

*Morley, H. T. *Old and Curious Playing Cards. Their History and Types from many Countries and Periods.* London. 1931. London. 8vo. Illustrated. 235 pages.

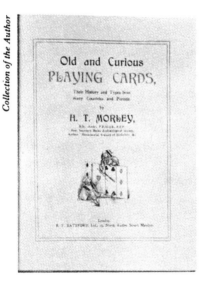

Collection of the Author

Title Page from *Old and Curious Playing Cards.* H. T. Morley. 1931.

> Includes a section on Tarocchi and Atout cards with the meanings of each of the Major Arcana cards.

*Mornand, Pierre. *Cartes et Tarots du Cabinet des Estampes.* France Illustration Magazine. France. Christmas 1946. Folio. Illustrated. Text in French. 17 pages.

A reproduction of old tarot cards in full color with text on the controversial origin of cards and their development throughout Europe.

*Muchery, Georges. *The Astrological Tarot (Astromancy)*. New York. (no date). 8vo. Illustrated. 312 pages.

Describes a system of divination combining the tarot pack and astrology. Utilizes a forty-eight-card pack which bears a descriptive title on each card as well as a symbolic picture.

*Nordic, Rolla. *The Tarot Shows The Path, Divination through the Tarot*. England. 1960. 12mo. Illustrated. 127 pages.

Describes each of the twenty-two Major Arcana cards, methods of divination, sample readings and methods of spreading the cards.

*O'Donoghue, Freeman. M. *Catalogue of The Collection of Playing Cards Bequeathed to the Trustees of the British Museum by the Late Lady Charlotte Schreiber*. London, 1901. 8vo. 228 pages.

Describes several hundred tarot packs, including Tarocchi, Tarocchino and Minchiate decks, in the Schreiber Collection. (See British Museum) Decks are from many countries including Italy, France, Germany, Switzerland, and Belgium.

*Orsini, Julia. *Le Grand Etteilla ou L'Art de Tirer les Cartes, contenant (1) Une introduction rappelant l'origine des cartes; (2) L'indication des tarots qui composent le véritable livre de Thot, avec la manière de les remplacer dans le cas ou l'on ne pourrait pas se les procurer; (3) Une méthode au moyen de laquelle on peut facilement apprendre soi-même sa destinée*, etc. Paris. (circa) 1800. 12mo. Illustrated. Text in French. 209 pages.

Describes the seventy-eight tarot cards of Etteilla

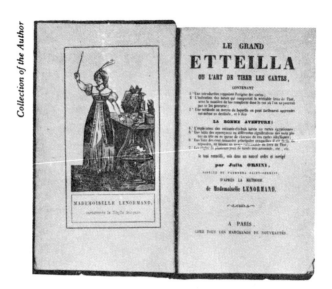

Frontispiece and Title Page from *Le Grand Etteilla ou L'Art de Tirer les Cartes*. Julia Orsini, Circa 1800.

including origin of the cards, significance and meaning of each card for divination, methods of spreading the cards, list of sample questions and rules of tarot games.

Papoli, Paolo. *L'Utile col diletto o sia Geografia Intrecciata nel Giuoco de Tarocchi con le Insegne Degl' Illustrissimi, ed Eccelsi Signori Gonfalonieri, ed Anziani di Bologna.* 1725. 24mo. Illustrated. 138 pages.

Describes a game of Tarocchi which contains busts of various personages or objects at the top section of each card and geographical lessons on the main body of the cards.

*Papus (Gerard Encausse). *The Tarot of the Bohemians. Absolute Key to Occult Science.* New York. 1970. Reprint. Illustrated. 352 pages.

A complete work describing Tarot codices and diagrams and summarizing the personal thesis of the author. Supports the Egyptian origin of cards as the most ancient book of the world.

* ———— . *Le Tarot Divinatoire: Clef du Tirage des Cartes et des Sorts.* Paris. 1909. Illustrated. Text in French.

The text includes a complete reconstitution of all the tarot symbols in a new design by which Papus believed new applications of divination were thus realized.

* ———— . *Traité Méthodique de Science Occulte.* Paris. 1891. 8vo. Text in French.

Includes a section on gypsies and a reproduction of the tarot pack after the indications of Oswald Wirth.

* ———— . *Traité Elémentaire de Science Occulte Mettant Chacun a Même de Comprendre et d'Expliquer Les Théories et Les Symboles Employés Par Les Anciens, Par Les Alchimistes, Les Francs-Maçons, etc.* Paris. 1888. 12mo. Illustrated. Text in French. 219 pages.

Elementary text on occult science including the ancient origins and methods employed.

* ———— . *La Kabbale. (Tradition Sécrète de L'Occident).* Résumé Méthodique. Paris. 1892. 8vo. Illustrated. Text in French. 188 pages.

Includes text on the divisions of the Kabbalah, the Sephiroth, the Hebrew alphabet, and an extensive bibliography.

*Phillips, Henry D. *Catalogue of The Collection of Playing Cards of Various Ages and Countries.* London. 1903. 8vo. 125 pages.

Describes various Tarot, Tarocchino and Minchiate packs owned by the British Museum. Printed for private circulation only.

*Pushong, Carlyle A. *The Tarot of the Magi.* London. 1967. 8vo. Illustrated. 111 pages.

Describes the meanings of each of the twenty-two Major Arcana cards, the sixteen court cards and four aces. Includes divinatory aspects of the tarot pack including the correspondence between the Hebrew alphabet, numerical power and astrological significance.

*Rákóczi, Basil Ivan. *The Painted Caravan: A Penetration Into the Secrets of the Tarot Cards.* Holland. 1954. 8vo. Illustrated. 119 pages.

Describes tarot history according to Gypsy lore, the meanings of the Major Arcana and Lesser Arcana cards, and techniques of divination.

*Ricci, Franco Maria. *Tarocchi Il Mazzo Visconteo di Bergamo e New York Analisi di Sergio Samek Ludovici. Testo di Italo Calvino (Il Castello dei destini incrociati).* Italy. 1969. Folio. Illustrated. Text in Italian. 165 pages.

Beautifully reproduced Tarocchi cards from the Visconti-Sforza deck. The cards are individually pasted on separate pages in the book with accompanying com-

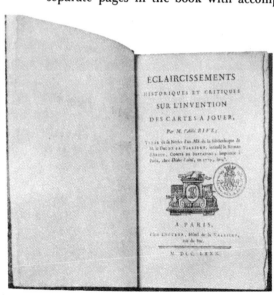

Collection of the Author

Title Page from *Eclaircissements Historiques et Critiques sur L'Invention des Cartes à Jouer.* M. l'Abbé Rive. 1780.

mentary about the cards and art work. Includes thirty-five cards presently owned by The Pierpont Morgan Library and twenty-six cards in the possession of the Accademia Carrara, Bergamo, Italy.

*Rive, M. l'Abbé. *Eclaircissements Historiques et Critiques Sur L'Invention des Cartes à Jouer.* Paris. 1780. 16mo. Text in French. 48 pages.

Only one hundred copies published. Relates the various nationalistic viewpoints regarding the possible European origin of playing cards in Germany, Spain, Italy and France as cited in sixty-five published references. Rare collector's item.

*S.M.R.D. & Others. *The Tarot Book: The Secret Workings of the Golden Dawn,* Book "T". England. 1967. 8vo. Illustrated. 149 pages.

Describes the seventy-eight tarot symbols together with their meanings. Assigns each card to the elements and zodialogical symbols.

*Sadhu, Mouni. *The Tarot. A Contemporary Course of The Quintessence of Hermetic Occultism.* London. 1968. 8vo. Illustrated. 494 pages.

Describes in a series of a hundred and one lessons, the twenty-two Major Arcana cards from the standpoints of symbolism, hermetism, numerology, relationship to the Hebrew alphabet and astrological relationships.

*Schreiber, W. L. *Die ältesten Spielkarten und die auf das Kartenspiel Bezug habenden Urkunden des 14. und 15. Jahrhunderts.* Germany. 1937. 8vo. Illustrated. Text in German. 176 pages.

Describes the oldest known playing cards and chronicles of the 14th and 15th centuries pertaining to card playing. Includes bibliography and dictionary of card playing terms.

*Seguin, Jean-Pierre. *Le Jeu de Carte.* Paris. 1968. 8vo. Illustrated. Text in French. 344 pages.

> An iconographic review of the history of playing cards and its techniques of production. In addition to rare documents, this book recounts the role played by the symbolic images.

*Seligmann, Kurt. *The Mirror of Magic. A History of Magic in The Western World.* Massachusetts. 1948. 8vo. Illustrated. 504 pages.

> Describes the tarot pack, pps. 409 to 434, including brief origin of the cards and divinatory meanings. Several different tarot packs are illustrated.

*Singer, Samuel Weller. *Researches into the History of Playing Cards with Illustrations of the Origin of Printing and Engraving on Wood.* London. 1816. 4to. Illustrated. 373 pages.

Collection of the Author

Frontispiece and Title Page from *Researches into the History of Playing Cards.* Samuel Weller Singer. 1816.

Only two hundred and fifty copies published. Extensive research into the history of playing cards including references to various possible origins of tarot cards. The Appendix includes: (1) Extracts from the Italian Poem on the game of Tarocco; (2) Reprint in French of Court de Gebelin's dissertation from *Le Monde Primitif: "Du Jeu des Tarots,* etc"; (3) Reprint of the work of M. L'Abbé Rive on the *"Ecclaircissements Historiques et Critiques sur l'Invention des Cartes à Jouer";* and (4) Reprint of *"Recherches Sur Les Tarots, et Sur La Divination Par Les Cartes des Tarots,* by M. Le C. de M. . . ." Very rare collector's item.

*Staatsgalerie Stuttgart. *Spielkarten aus aller Welt vom Mittelalter bis zur Gegenwart, aus dem Museum der Vereinigten Altenburger und Stralsunder Spielkartenfabriken, Leinfelden bei Stuttgart, und aus deutschen Sammlungen.* Stuttgart. 1968. Folio. Illustrated. Text in German. 104 pages.

Contains description of cards including tarots on display at exhibits from September 6 to November 3, 1968 at the Staatsgalerie in Stuttgart. Includes several full color reproductions of tarot cards.

*Steiger, Brad and Ron Warmoth. *The Tarot.* New York. 1969. 16mo. Illustrated. 168 pages.

Describes in story form methods of divination using the complete tarot deck.

*Taylor, Rev. Ed. S. *The History of Playing Cards with Anecdotes of their Use in Conjuring, Fortune-Telling, and Card-Sharping.* London. 1865. 16mo. Illustrated. 529 pages.

Describes the history of playing cards and the introduction of cards into various European countries.

Includes a chapter on early cartomancy and fortune-telling. Published posthumously and is practically a translation of the earlier work by P. Boiteau D'Ambly.

Title Page from
*The History of
Playing Cards.*
Rev. Ed. S. Taylor.
1865.

*Thierens, A. E. *The General Book of the Tarot.* Containing the Astrological Key to the Tarot-system. Pennsylvania. 1928. 8vo. 158 pages.

Describes the doctrine of the tarot pack and the significance of each of the twenty-two Major Arcana and fifty-six Lesser Arcana cards including astrological keys.

*Tilley, Roger. *Playing Cards.* New York. 1967. 8vo. Illustrated. 120 pages.

Includes description of early playing cards including Tarot and Minchiate packs.

*Trismégiste, J. *Manuel Illustre de Cartomancie. L'Art de Tirer Les Cartes Français suivi du Livre de Thot ou Jeu de la Princesse Tarot.* Paris. 1867. 24mo. Illustrated. Text in French. 192 pages.

Describes a tarot pack with Egyptian influenced designs. Includes methods of reading the cards and significance of each card.

*Vaillant, J. A. *Les Rômes, histoire vraie des vrais Bohémiens.* Paris. 1857. 8vo.

Includes descriptions of the Major Arcana cards and seeks to show that tarot designs are heirlooms of the highest conceptions of Hindustani wisdom.

*Van Rensselaer, Mrs. John King. *The Devil's Picture Books. A History of Playing Cards.* New York. 1895. 8vo. Illustrated. 207 pages.

Presents a history of playing cards including a brief section on the tarot pack.

* ———— . *Prophetical Educational and Playing Cards.* Philadelphia. 1912. 8vo. Illustrated. 392 pages.

Traces the history of tarot cards from the Egyptian Mercury and seeks to prove the origin of cards from ancient mysteries.

*Waite, Arthur Edward. *The Key to the Tarot. Being Fragments of a Secret Tradition under the Veil of Divination.* London. 1920. Reprint. 24mo. 212 pages.

Deals with the antiquities of tarot cards, the symbolism of each card as defined by Waite in his modern pack, a study of the various methods of divination and a description of several spreads.

* ———— *The Holy Kabbalah.* A Study of the Secret Tradition in Israel as unfolded by Sons of the Doctrine for the Benefit and Consolation of the Elect dispersed through the Lands and Ages of The Greater Exile. New

York. 1960. Reprint. 8vo. 636 pages.

Introduction to the mysteries of the Kabbalah. Presents a comprehensive history of the origins, meanings and applications of the doctrines of the Kabbalah.

*Williams, Charles. *The Greater Trumps*. London. 1964. Reprinted. 12mo. 230 pages.

The twenty-two Major Arcana cards are described in a story of modern times.

*Willshire, William Hughes. *A Descriptive Catalogue of Playing And Other Cards in the British Museum accompanied by a Concise General History of the Subject and Remarks on Cards of Divination and of a Politico-Historical Character*. London. 1876. 4to. Illustrated. 360 pages.

Contains summary of some of the popular viewpoints regarding the origin and occult development of tarot cards and a description of some tarot packs in the British Museum. Supplement with illustrations, 1877. 87 pages.

*Wirth, Oswald. *Le Tarot, des Imagiers du Moyen Age*. Paris. 1969. Reprint. 8vo. Text in French. 374 pages.

Describes the history of tarot cards in support of Egyptian origin, the meaning and symbolism of each card as defined by Wirth in modified pictures bearing the appropriate letter of the Hebrew alphabet, and discusses methods of interpretation and divination. Includes pack of twenty-two Major Arcana cards in sleeve at back of book.

*Zain, C. C. *The Sacred Tarot*. Los Angeles. 1969. 16mo. Illustrated. 416 pages.

This volume actually comprises 13 serials including chronology of tarot, how to read the tarot, scope and use of the tarot, and the sacred tarot as a doctrine of Kabbalism.

Glossary

Acorns Suit sign equivalent to clubs (German).

Allegorical cards The twenty-two Major Arcana cards from the tarot deck which bear pictorial and symbolic representations.

Altenburger Und Stralsunder Well-known German manufactuer of playing cards descended from a number of 19th-century firms and located at Leinfelden.

Arcana Taken from the Italian *arcano* meaning secret or esoteric knowledge. (Latin - *arcanum*).

Atouts French for the twenty-two Major Arcana or trump cards in the tarot deck.

Atutti Italian for the twenty-two Major Arcana or trump cards in the tarot deck.

Back design Designs appearing on the backs of cards. Some early cards were blank.

Bastoni Suit sign equivalent to clubs (Italian).

Batons Suit sign equivalent to clubs (French).

Carreaux Suit sign of paving tiles equivalent to diamonds (French).

Cartier Name given to French card-makers in late 16th century.

Cartomancy The art of using cards for any means of fortune-telling.

Cavalier Court card located between the Queen and Jack in the Tarot deck (French).

Chalice Suit sign equivalent to hearts (French).

Chaturange Oriental game of chess dating from the fifth or sixth century in India.

Chevalier Court card located between the Queen and Jack in the tarot deck (French).

Coat cards Picture or court cards were originally called coat cards because the King, Queen, and Knave were dressed in costumes or coats.

Coins Suit sign equivalent to diamonds.

Coeurs Suit sign equivalent to hearts (French).

Coppes Suit sign equivalent to hearts (Italian).

Court cards The King, Queen, Knight, and Page in each of the four suits of the tarot pack.

Cudgels Suit sign equivalent to clubs.

Cups Suit sign equivalent to hearts.

Dame Court card equivalent to Queen (French).

Denari Suit sign equivalent to diamonds (Italian).

Divination Fortune-telling or prophesizing by various means including but not limited to playing cards.

Diviner A person who reads and interprets the card spread for the purpose of reading the future.

Double-headed courts The picture on the court card is double-headed and may be viewed from either end. With few rare exceptions, double-headed court cards were not used in England or the United States before 1850. Other European countries used double-headed courts at an earlier date, about the first quarter of the 19th century; some Italian decks even earlier.

Emblematical cards The twenty-two Major Arcana cards from the tarot pack which bear pictorial and symbolic representations.

Epées Suit sign equivalent to spades (French).

Fournier, S. A. Well-known Spanish manufacturer of playing cards originating in the 19th century and located at Vitorio.

Frame line Outer line framing the back design of the card. If the frame line is square-cornered, then generally the card is square-cornered; if it is round-cornered, then the likelihood exists that the card was round-cornered to start with.

Greater Arcana The twenty-two emblematical and symbolic picture cards in the tarot pack.

Grimaud, B.P. Well-known French manufacturer of playing cards originating in the 18th century and located in Paris. Recently acquired by J.M. Simon/France Cartes who is continuing the Grimaud product line.

Hand-painted The earliest known tarot cards were painted by hand on heavy cardboard.

Hand-stenciled 18th and 19th century tarot cards were generally hand-colored by using seperate stencils for each color and applying color with brushes or rollers.

Hawk-bells Suit sign equivalent to diamonds (German).

Indices Letters or numbers found in the corners of each card and used to identify the card without fanning out the entire hand. This practice was adopted in the latter part of the 19th century. Different countries used different letters to identify the court cards. For example, (England and the United States) K, Q, J, A; (France) R, D, C, V, A, or I.

Kabbalah Ancient occult theosophy widely transmitted in medieval Europe and based upon esoteric interpretations of the Hebrew scriptures.

Knave Court card equivalent to Jack (French).

Knight Court card located between the Queen and Jack in the tarot deck.

Layout Card spread used for reading the tarot cards.

Leaves Suit sign equivalent to spades (German).

Lesser Arcana Fifty-six cards comprising fourteen cards in each of the four suits from King to Ace or one.

Major Arcana The twenty-two emblematic and symbolic picture cards in the tarot pack.

Maker The person or company publishing the pack of cards. Almost all cards have at least one card upon which appears the maker's name and address.

Minchiate cards Minchiate of Florence decks comprise ninety-seven cards and are similar to tarot packs.

Minor Arcana Fifty-six cards comprising fourteen cards in each of the four suits from King to Ace or one.

Money Suit sign equivalent to diamonds.

Muller & Cie Well-known Swiss manufacturer of playing cards originating in the early 19th century and located at Neuhausen Am Rheinfall.

Muller 1JJ Deck Famous 1JJ Tarot pack produced by Muller & Cie. The initials "JJ" stand for the two Major Arcana cards, Junon and Jupiter.

Numeral cards The forty cards in the Lesser Arcana of the tarot pack which are numbered from 10 through 1 or Ace in each of the four suits.

Obermann Court card equivalent to Queen (German).

Pack The complete seventy-eight-card tarot deck.

Pentacles Suit sign equivalent to diamonds (French).

Piatnik, Ferd & Sohne Well-known Austrian manufacturer of playing cards originating about 1824 and located in Vienna.

Piedmontese tarot Seventy-eight-card tarot pack with French inscriptions originating from an area near Bologna.

Pip cards Cards numbered 10 through 1 in each of the four suits.

Piques Suit sign of pike heads equivalent to spades (French).

Querent The person seeking an answer to a question through means of cartomancy, also known as the questioner.

Reader The person who interprets the spread of the cards in order to foretell the future, also known as the diviner.

Revenue stamp The tax stamp appearing on some cards and/or card wrappers which helps to identify the country of origin and date of the pack of cards.

Rider Waite deck Famous seventy-eight-card tarot deck designed by Pamela Colman Smith under the direction of Arthur Edward Waite.

Roi Court card equivalent to King (French).

Round-corners Round-cornered cards appeared for the first time around the end of the 19th century.

Scepters Suit sign equivalent to clubs (French).

Sephiroth The ten fundamental truths to which are connected the twenty-two Paths of Life in the Kabbalah.

Significator The cards selected to typify or signify the questioner.

Spade Suit sign equivalent to spades (Italian).

Spread The manner in which the tarot cards are laid out for the purpose of reading the cards.

Square-corners Square-cornered cards were commonplace prior to 1890.

Suits The four suits comprising the Minor Arcana cards, usually known as swords (spades), wands (clubs), cups (hearts), and pentacles (diamonds).

Taroc Game of tarot as known in Austria. Also spelled tarok and tarock.

Tarocchi of Mantegna The Montegna deck comprises fifty instructive cards in five classes of ten cards each.

Tarocchi deck The Tarocchi of Venice or Lombardi deck comprises seventy-eight cards.

Tarocchino deck The Tarocchino of Bologna deck comprises sixty-two cards. It is reputed to have been invented by Francois Fibbia.

Tarot deck The complete seventy-eight-card fortune-telling deck comprising twenty-two Major Arcana cards and fifty-six Lesser Arcana cards.

Tarot Classic deck Famous seventy-eight-card tarot deck based upon Claude Burdel designs from the 18th century, and produced by Muller & Cie, Switzerland.

Tarot of Marseilles deck Famous seventy-eight-card tarot pack produced by B. P. Grimaud since the 19th century.

Tarotée Term applied to the back design of early cards bearing a multiple series of crisscrossing lines.

Tarotiers Name given to Cartiers in Paris in the latter part of the 16th century.

Tarotrump game Currently a popular seventy-eight-card tarot game based upon ancient rules of the 16th century Italian games of Minchiate and Tarocchi.

Tax stamp Revenue stamps sometimes used to control production of playing cards and to obtain revenue for the country in which production takes place.

Tree of Life Taken from the Kabbalah and comprising the ten Sephiroth and the twenty-two connecting Paths, numbered from 11-32.

Trefles Suit sign of trefoils or clover equivalent to clubs (French).

Trumps The twenty-two Major Arcana cards.

Untermann Court card equivalent to Jack (German).

Valet Court card equivalent to Jack (French).

Wands Suit sign equivalent to clubs.

Index